FINANCIAL APPRAISAL

UNIT 2

UNDERSTANDING ACCOUNTS

Financial Strategy

Prepared for the Course Team by Patricia Swannell
with contributions by Clare Minchington and Graham Francis

The Open University

BUSINESS

SCHOOL

OPEN UNIVERSITY COURSE TEAM

Core Group

Professor Janette Rutterford, *Production and Presentation Course Team Co-Chair and Author*

Bernardo Batiz-Lazo, *Presentation Course Team Co-Chair and Author*

David Barnes

Marcus Davison, *Author*

Graham Francis, *Author*

Carmel de Nahlik, *Author*

Jan Gadella, *Author*

Margaret Greenwood

Heinz Kassier

Tony Anthoni, *Course Manager*

Carmel McMahon

Clare Minchington, *Author*

Kathy Reay, *Course Team Assistant*

Pat Sucher, *Author*

Patricia Swannell, *Author*

Richard Wheatcroft, *Author*

External Assessor

Professor Paul Draper, *Walter Scott and Partners Professor of Finance, University of Edinburgh*

Production Team

Sylvan Bentley, *Picture Researcher*

John Bradley, *Design Group Co-ordinator*

Martin Brazier, *Graphic Designer*

Jenny Edwards, *Product Quality Assistant*

Anne Faulkner, *Information Specialist*

John Garne, *Computing Consultant*

Roy Lawrance, *Graphic Artist*

David Libbert, *BBC Series Producer*

Richard Mole, *Director of Production OUBS*

Henry Dougherty, *Editor*

Kathy Reay, *Course Team Assistant*

Linda K. Smith, *Project Controller*

Doreen Tucker, *Compositor*

Christine Villas-Boas, *Computing Consultant*

Steve Wilkinson, *BBC Series Producer*

External Critical Readers

Stephen Abbott

George Buckberry

Linda Cinderey

Roland Davis

Angela Garrett

Jane Hughes

Ed Hutt

Rosemary F. Johnson

Geoff Jones

Robin Joy

David Kirk

Archie McArthur

Richard Mischak

Professor Chris Napier

Eugene Power

Manvinder Singh

Tony Whitford

The Open University, Walton Hall, Milton Keynes MK7 6AA

First published 1998. Second edition 1999. Third edition 2000. Reprinted 2001

Copyright © 1998, 1999, 2000 The Open University

Edited, designed and typeset by The Open University

Printed and bound in the United Kingdom by The Burlington Press (Cambridge) Ltd.

ISBN 0 7492 9726 3

Further information on Open University Business School courses may be obtained from the Course Sales Development Centre, The Open University, PO Box 222, Milton Keynes MK7 6YY (Telephone: 01908 653449).

22882B/b821b2u2i3.2

CONTENTS

1 INTRODUCTION

1.1 INTRODUCTION TO THE BLOCK

The aim of this very practical block is to give you the skills that will allow you to read an Annual Report and Accounts and draw conclusions about:

- the financial issues facing the company's management
- the creditworthiness of the company from the point of view of lenders or trading partners
- the attractions of the company to existing and potential investors.

Note that this unit and the next one deal almost exclusively with the commercial sector.

The skills considered in this block are important tools for identifying the strategic options that are available to a company and for monitoring progress towards strategic goals. Unit 2 focuses on the tools used in the analysis of a company's *historical* performance while Unit 3 concentrates on how the assessment of historical performance may be used to anticipate *future* performance.

Throughout the block, you will see how analysts within a company, or from banks and other organisations in the financial sector, look at financial data for decision-making purposes. You will find that, by the end of the block, you will no longer find a company's Annual Report and Accounts intimidating. Instead, you will have a clear understanding of how to extract relevant financial information from a set of accounts in order to make a particular type of decision, whether it be to forecast future cash flows for a company valuation or to assess financing needs from an internal or external perspective.

The approach we adopt in this block is to introduce you to the key financial statistics in an Annual Report and Accounts and show how these can be analysed in the form of financial ratios. The attraction of ratios is that they allow the analyst to study the performance of a company over time and to compare its performance with that of other, competing, companies. Historical ratios are also indispensable for forecasting future performance in a way which is consistent with past performance.

The prominent role of ratio analysis in evaluating a company's performance and its management was confirmed in a statement issued following the replacement of the Chief Executive of the large UK glass maker, Pilkington plc. In announcing the change, the chairman, Nigel Rudd, commented, '... the pace of change was not fast enough. Compared with our competitors, Pilkington's ratios were not as good. I did not think that was acceptable.' (*Daily Telegraph*, 22 May 1997)

Units 2 and 3 take you slowly but surely through a company's Annual Report and Accounts. Numerous real examples are used throughout this block, from the UK and elsewhere, to help highlight the importance of particular ratios. Financial issues are placed in the context of strategy. As you will have seen in B820, and as Unit 1 reminded you, there is a close link between strategy and finance – hence the name of this course!

In Unit 2, we introduce you to a UK company, Blue Circle Industries plc (Blue Circle) and in Unit 3 to another UK company, The Boots Company plc (Boots). These will be referred to from time to time throughout the rest of the course, enabling you to see how the different aspects of financial strategy fit together. In this block, you will use Blue Circle as the main case study for your exercises. You also encounter it in the context of

You will find the OUFS useful in your work for analysing *any* organisation you feel like dissecting.

your first Excel spreadsheet on the course, the Open University Financial Spreadsheet (OUFS), a complete financial analysis package which will automatically calculate a broad range of financial ratios, taking much of the mechanical work out of the financial exercises in this block.

At the end of this block, you should have a system which allows you to distil the relevant facts from this wealth of information in order to reach conclusions about an organisation from a variety of perspectives.

1.2   INTRODUCTION TO THE UNIT

As we will see in this unit, the wealth of information included in an Annual Report and Accounts can best be digested through the systematic examination of various types of information in turn. In this way, we ensure we omit nothing and also that we are able to make comparisons across organisations. After an introductory section, therefore, this unit follows the same sequence of analysis that should be used to examine the financial information provided in an Annual Report in an efficient way, whatever the ultimate use of the analysis. As we go through the analysis, we highlight which financial statistics and ratios are most relevant to each type of user.

You have received CD-ROM 1 'Foundations of Financial Analysis'. We have provided this disk for you to refresh your knowledge of basic accounting, for this course.

Financial analysis is fairly straightforward in practice, requiring a thorough and consistent approach, a basic understanding of accounting and, most important of all, the application of common sense to the results!

The rewards for being able to carry out a financial analysis on a company can be great. A salutary example is provided by the UK firm, Queens Moat Houses plc, which caused both its lenders and investors to lose a great deal of money (see Box 1.1).

BOX 1.1   QUEENS MOAT HOUSES PLC

Queens Moat is a company listed on the London Stock Exchange which operated a chain of 160 hotels in 1993. Queens Moat shares were suspended in March 1993 following the announcement of substantial losses. Only a few months earlier, a group of major international banks had agreed large new loans to the company. The factors that brought about the inevitable and dramatic collapse in profits were clearly set out in the Annual Report and Accounts, which were readily available to the banks when they made their decision to lend. If only these bankers had had access to this course!

For 20 years prior to 1993, Queens Moat had been operating an unconventional management incentive programme. Each manager in the scheme was called upon to agree a revenue stream with the parent company, signing a promissory note guaranteeing these payments. If a manager's hotel did not generate enough revenue to make these payments, the manager was called upon to make up the shortfall. If a hotel generated revenues in excess of the agreed figure, this excess was retained by the manager. The scheme was designed to give managers greater autonomy to improve their profits as well as to reduce central management overheads.

The promissory notes signed by the managers were taken into the accounts when they were agreed. This meant that the company accounts reflected revenues that would not be collected until as much as one year later. The company was, in effect, including next year's forecast revenues as the current year's sales figure. Problems arose when the UK economy went into recession: managers found that they were unable to meet their agreed targets, but had no wealth to meet their obligations under their promissory notes.

The effect of this unusual incentive programme was that Queens Moat had accounts receivable which were outstanding on average many months longer than was the case in other hotel chains. As sales, and hence profits, were entered into the accounts long before cash was received – even assuming that the forecast sales were likely to be achieved – Queens Moat had had difficulty finding cash to pay lenders and investors as early as 1990. The abnormal level of accounts receivable and the cash deficit which had been apparent since 1990, *should* have alerted the lending banks and shareholders to the unconventional incentive programme and to Queens Moat's impending financial difficulties. The information was available in print but its significance was not recognised. By applying the methods you will learn in this unit, the lending banks could have saved themselves millions of pounds in bad debts. You can read the 'Notes to the Accounts' relating to the restatement of the accounts following the restructuring of the group as Case Study 8 in the Course Reader.

This course will use International Accounting Standards Committee (IASC) terminology and definitions which are being increasingly used in both the UK and overseas.

Outline of Unit 2

Section 2, 'Why Annual Reports?', outlines the scope and focus of the unit and considers some basic differences between accounting policies in different countries. Section 3, 'Analysis in context', focuses on analysing the sector in which the company operates. It is here that we see a further link between strategy and finance. Section 4, 'Operating efficiency', looks at operating efficiency ratios, those ratios which help the analyst assess the efficiency with which a company manages its assets. Section 5, 'Financial structure', examines how to assess the financial structure of a company, by looking at solvency and liquidity ratios. Section 6, 'Profitability', considers the consequences of the operating and financing decisions as reflected in the profitability ratios. Section 7, 'Ratio analysis', looks at how the asset efficiency, solvency and profitability ratios interconnect through the core ratios to give an overall picture of the financial performance of a company. Finally, Section 8, 'Cash flow', focuses on the derivation and analysis of a company's cash flow and considers how, in many cases (including that of Queens Moat!), cash flow may be a more relevant measure of performance than accounting **profit** or earnings.

Aims and objectives of the unit

By the end of this unit, you should be able to:

- monitor the efficiency of a company over time and relative to competitors
- be aware of strategic options and monitor, through financial analysis, the progress a company has made towards achieving its strategic goals
- choose reliable suppliers and customers, or trading partners for your own organisation
- avoid unprofitable investments!

2 WHY ANNUAL REPORTS?

This section considers why understanding accounts is an important skill. It also explains how you can approach the daunting task of evaluating a company on the basis of the wealth of information included in an Annual Report. Annual Reports vary from country to country and this section will explain why we have chosen to focus on accounts prepared on an Anglo-American model using International Accounting Standards terminology. The content of an annual report will be reviewed and we will introduce the Open University Financial Spreadsheet (OUFS) which allows you to transfer financial information to a standard format and automatically calculate(s) a range of ratios. Finally, we set out the sequence of analysis we follow to draw conclusions about a company on the basis of information published in an Annual Report.

2.1 WHO NEEDS THE ANNUAL REPORT?

The Annual Report and Accounts (Annual Report) is the principal means of communicating with the outside world for companies whose shares are traded publicly. Not-for-profit organisations generally also produce Annual Reports to inform supervisory bodies and contributors. Regardless of the job you do, it is very likely that at some point you will join one of the following stakeholder categories:

- *investors* needing to choose and monitor investments
- *lenders* needing to confirm and monitor a borrower's ability to pay interest and repay debt
- *managers* needing to judge the financial strength of a potential trading partner and monitor the health of existing suppliers and customers
- *contributors* to a not-for-profit organisation wanting to confirm the appropriate use of your contribution
- *managers of public companies* needing to prepare information for the providers of equity, debt and trade credit
- *employees of public companies* interested in the financial health of their employer.

'Would you please instruct Collins not to roll his eyes when I read the financial report.'

As a member of any of these categories, you will need to read Annual Reports and make judgements based on the information presented in them.

2.2 WHICH ANNUAL REPORTS?

The form and content of an Annual Report will vary from country to country according to the rules laid down by bodies such as accounting standards boards or stock exchanges, or reflecting national statutes. Although there are wide variations in form and practice throughout the world, it is possible to divide national accounting and reporting requirements in the developed world into two very broad categories of countries which share the same general approach:

(i) Countries following the Anglo-American model (often referred to as the 'Anglo-Saxon' model) which seeks to set out a 'fair' view of a company's performance and financial position in a given year from the point of view of the shareholders.

(ii) Countries following the Franco-German model, reflecting the precedence of creditors' interests, and the requirement that accounts prepared for shareholders must be the same as those prepared for the tax authorities. The 'creditor' perspective encourages greater conservatism in recognising both income and expenses: *profits* may be entered into the accounts only when they have been realised, while expected *losses/expenses* may be entered into the accounts immediately. As a consequence of this greater conservatism, profits tend to be recognised later in these countries.

Recognising profits *later* does not mean having to *have* profits – as Daimler-Benz showed in 1994 when it reported losses under US accounting standards which had been profits under German standards! (See Section 6.1.)

The New York Stock Exchange and (to a lesser extent) the London Stock Exchange represent important sources of equity funding for international companies. Any company wishing to gain access to these funds is obliged to meet their standards of reporting and disclosure. US, UK or International Accounting Standards, all of which follow the Anglo-American approach, are being increasingly adopted by international companies (including those headquartered in countries within the Franco-German block) that need access to these financial markets (Waller, 1996). We will therefore focus primarily on accounts prepared on the basis of the Anglo-American model. It is important to recognise differences do exist even within the Anglo-American model in reporting standards. Where the Franco-German model contrasts with the Anglo-American model, this will be highlighted.

Table 2.1 sets out the models that underlie the accounting approaches of the major developed countries.

Table 2.1 Accounting models in major developed countries	
Anglo-American Model	**Franco-German Model**
Australia	Austria
Canada	Belgium
India	Finland
Ireland	France
Netherlands	Germany
New Zealand	Greece
United Kingdom	Italy
United States of America	Japan
	Luxembourg
	Norway
	Portugal
	Spain
	Sweden
	Switzerland

Activity 2.1

Read the article by Ball in the Course Reader. This offers a framework for categorising accounting differences among countries.

2.3 WHAT TERMINOLOGY?

Also be aware that words in common English usage may have very specific accounting meaning.

Accounting terminology varies from jurisdiction to jurisdiction and can be very confusing. In some instances, the same word can have different meanings in different jurisdictions (for example, the term 'stock' in UK accounts means 'goods held for resale', while in US accounts it means equity capital). In the hope of minimising potential confusion, we will use IASC accounting terminology as defined in the IASC Accounting Glossary in the course Glossary.

The cases and illustrations which are included in Units 2 and 3 are primarily medium to large corporations, since the tools which we are outlining are most applicable to such companies. They are, nonetheless, useful tools for companies of any size. In the case of small organisations it is also crucial to assess the skills of the key personnel. In the case of not-for-profit or public-sector companies (such as housing associations or UK National Health Trusts) these same tools can be adapted and extended to include output-related performance indicators.

2.4 CONTENTS OF THE ANNUAL REPORT

An Annual Report following the Anglo-American model can be divided between those sections required by law, the compulsory sections, and those voluntary sections included to give a clearer and less technical interpretation of the company's recent performance and future prospects.

Compulsory Sections

The following sections must be included in the Annual Reports of a company, and are subject to inspection and report by the Company's auditors.

(i) the directors' report

(ii) the auditors' report

(iii) the income statement

(iv) the balance sheet

(v) the cashflow statement

(vi) notes to the accounts

Voluntary sections

(i) the chairman's statement

(ii) the chief executive's review

(iii) the operating and financial review (OFR)

(iv) the environmental report

These optional reports are relatively new innovations and their content is not specified. However, they provide a rich source of information, even if that information is usually provided in the most favourable light for the company.

We will now describe the compulsory sections of the Annual Report in more detail. The last four compulsory sections in the list above, the income statement, the balance sheet, the cashflow statement and the notes to the accounts, which provide the hard financial statistics, will be considered together in the subsection entitled 'Financial statements and related notes'.

The directors' report

The content of the directors' report is specified in the UK by the law and also by Stock Exchange requirements.

In both the USA and the UK, listed companies must now include a statement on corporate governance. In the UK, this is linked to the 'combined Code-Principles of Good Governance and Code of Best Practice' published in June 1998 which brought together the work of the Cadbury, Greenbury and Hampel Committees.

Additional voluntary information about the company is, at present, normally included in the voluntary sections. The directors' report is therefore a rather dry and utilitarian section.

BOX 2.1 TWO VIEWS

It is instructive to compare the comments on trading conditions made by two chairmen of major UK retailers for similar periods:

Sir Richard Greenbury, Chairman, Marks and Spencer plc, commenting on the year ended 31 March 1996:

'I am pleased to report continued sales and profit growth with considerable physical expansion and development of the business both within the UK and overseas. [...]

'In the United Kingdom the very warm autumn weather resulted in some increase in the cost of post-Christmas reductions on clothing but we traded well throughout the rest of the year and maintained our market share. After several years in which home furnishings sales suffered from the stagnation in the housing market, this division staged a marked recovery.'

Sir Bob Reid, Chairman, Sears plc, commenting on the year ended 31 January 1996:

'There are few more competitive arenas than a British high street. A year of progressive, if erratic, recovery from economic recession has produced ample evidence of that. For Sears, 1995 was a year of immense change as we met the challenge of focusing our activities on key businesses, condensing our portfolio of brands from 24 to 11. [...] I have to report that the costs associated with the broad rationalisation programme coupled with shoppers' continued spending resistance exerted a negative impact on our financial results.'

Activity 2.2

Compare the presentation and content of the voluntary and compulsory sections of the Blue Circle 1997 Annual Report and Accounts which came with your course materials.

The auditors' report

The auditors' reports in Anglo-American Annual Reports normally follow a standard form stating that:

- the accounts have been audited to ensure appropriate accounting policies have been consistently applied and adequately disclosed
- the accounts present a 'fair' view of the company during the financial year and at the financial year-end
- the accounts have been prepared in accordance with the relevant legislation.

You must read the auditor's report to ensure that nothing is out of the ordinary, in particular that it is not 'qualified' in some way. Accounts may be qualified for a wide range of reasons which may be crucial to the assessment of the company.

In the UK, the auditors' opinion may be qualified if the auditors feel there has been a limitation to the scope of the audit or if they disagree with the treatment or disclosure of some matter. Alternatively, they may give a clear adverse opinion stating that the financial statements do not give a true and fair view or that they are unable to express an opinion. They may also cite some shortcoming and state that the financial statements give a true and fair view except for the specified shortcoming.

Where there is a situation of fundamental uncertainty that has been disclosed and accounted for appropriately, the auditors may include an explanation of the uncertainty but state that the opinion is not qualified.

BOX 2.2 THE AUDITORS' REPORT – UNQUALIFIED

A careful reading of the precise wording of the auditors' report can provide crucial information for the analyst. The explanatory paragraphs from the auditors' reports for Guinness Peat Aviation (GPA) and Eurotunnel – two companies that survived severe financial difficulties in the early 1990s – illustrate the information that may be provided by the auditors' report. Note that in both cases the auditors' report was not qualified.

Auditors' Report to the Members of GPA Group PLC

Fundamental Uncertainties – Going Concern

In forming our opinion we have considered the adequacy of the disclosures made in the financial statements concerning the validity of the going concern basis of preparation of the financial statements. This is dependent on:

(i) the successful implementation of the remaining aspects of the comprehensive restructuring programme agreed in October 1993,

(ii) the ability of GPA to generate adequate liquidity (including its ability to achieve aircraft sales) to enable it to meet its debt, aircraft purchase and other obligations in the period to September 1996,

(iii) the ability of GPA to put new financing arrangements in place by September 1996 to deal with the requirement to repay both the principal secured lenders and other lenders, and to enable GPA to meet its remaining aircraft purchase and other obligations thereafter and avoid penalties for contract cancellation, which ability may be dependent on the exercise by GE Capital of the GE Capital Option over a majority of the total voting rights in the company; and

(iv) the outcome of other fundamental uncertainties set out below.

The Directors are currently uncertain as to the outcome of these matters. The validity of the going concern basis on which the financial statements have been prepared depends on the successful conclusion of these matters. If the Company or its subsidiary undertakings were unable to continue in operational existence for the foreseeable future, substantial but unquantifiable adjustments would have to be made to reduce the balance sheet values of assets to their recoverable amounts, and to provide for further liabilities that might arise. Additionally, further adjustments would have to be made to reclassify fixed assets and long term liabilities as current assets and liabilities.

Details relating to these fundamental uncertainties are described in Note 1 and related notes. Our opinion is not qualified in this respect.

Fundamental Uncertainties – Other

In forming our opinion we have also considered the adequacy of the disclosures made in the financial statements concerning the following fundamental uncertainties:

(i)   The outcome of material litigation between GPA and McDonnell Douglas Corporation ('MDC') which, even if in the event it did not affect the going concern basis of accounting, could have a material effect on GPA's financial position.

(ii) GPA's ability to reach satisfactory arrangements with certain engine manufacturers and/or meet specified future purchase volume requirements so that the amounts already received relating to engine credits will not become repayable and further liabilities will not arise.

(iii) GPA's ability under the transactions with GE Capital to realise the full amount of the deferred payments (less provisions which have been made at March 31, 1994).

(iv) The value of GPA's investment in associated undertakings is dependent upon their continuation as going concerns.

The Directors are uncertain as to the outcome of these matters and details relating to these fundamental uncertainties are described in Note 1 and related notes. Our opinion is not qualified in these respects.

Auditors' Report – Eurotunnel P.L.C. Group

Going Concern

In forming our opinion, we have considered the adequacy of the disclosures made in Note 1 of the financial statements concerning the uncertainty over the validity of the going concern basis. This is dependent upon:

- the successful outcome of the negotiations with the syndicate of banks leading to a restructuring plan. The plan needs to demonstrate that the financing structure is matched to the existing and projected trading circumstances and requires to be approved within the standstill period. In the absence of a successful outcome of these negotiations, the banks could initiate the exercise of their security including their right of substitution;

- the receipt of any shareholder approval and additional financing or refinancing which may be required under the terms of the restructuring plan;

- trading operations to progress to a point at which the Eurotunnel Group becomes cash generative net of funding costs.

The financial statements do not include any adjustments that would result from any of the above issues not being successfully achieved or which might be required as a result of the terms of any restructuring plan. In view of the significance of this uncertainty we consider that it should be drawn to your attention but our opinion is not qualified in this respect.

Countries using the Franco-German model often do not require accounts to be audited, but depend on tax inspectors to ensure compliance. As organisations are taxed at the operating level, tax inspectors focus at that level and there is often no independent view on how the operating subsidiaries are 'added together' to form the consolidated accounts. This provides the scope for regular changes to accounting policy reflected in consolidated accounts, for example to address public relations considerations or to flatter performance, a characteristic of which all users should be aware.

The financial statements and related notes

The remaining four sections of the Annual Report include the bulk of the financial statistics and it is to these that we now direct our attention. The **income statement** summarises the company's productive activity during the year and can focus on sales during the year (Anglo-American model) or total production (an option under the Franco-German model).

The **balance sheet** summarises the position of the company at the end of the financial year. In jurisdictions where companies can choose the date of the end of their financial year, users must keep in mind that they may select the date at which their balance sheet looks most attractive. This will be at the 'low point' or the end of the production cycle in a seasonal company, when the cash for the year's production has been collected.

A **cash flow** statement may be provided to summarise the sources of cash and its uses during the year. Cash flow statements are included in the Annual Reports of larger companies in some jurisdictions and provide valuable information. Where a cash flow statement is not provided it is possible to estimate, or derive, a cash flow from the balance sheet and income statement, a process we outline in Section 8.

The **notes to the accounts** are a crucially important section for the user to consider in detail. They contain a wealth of detailed information that generally also appears in a summarised form in other sections of the Annual Report and they are indispensable to the user. While the importance of the information in the notes to the accounts cannot be overemphasised, this information should be considered to be an integral part of the balance sheet, income statement and cash flow statement; each of these must be considered in conjunction with the additional information which is presented in the associated notes.

Experienced analysts generally begin the process of assessing a company by taking information from several years of its Annual Reports and putting the financial statistics in a standard form, usually a computer-based spreadsheet. There are several good reasons why:

*   A particular item of information is more easily located in a standard form than a company form. (The form of published accounts varies considerably from company to company and from year to year in the same company.)
*   Several years of information can be viewed together so trends are readily identifiable.
*   Supplementary information which is disclosed only in the notes to the accounts can be highlighted (for example, raw material, work in progress and finished goods can be shown instead of the single category, **inventory**).
*   Financial ratios can be calculated automatically using consistent definitions and methodology, making comparison among companies and within companies over time easier .

The process may initially seem time-consuming. You will find, however, that the time you invest in extracting the information and inputting it into the Open University Financial Spreadsheet (OUFS) will be more than matched by the time you save in repeated searches through the masses of published information and hand calculation of financial ratios.

A hard copy of OUFS is given as Appendix 1 to this unit, and is on CDROM2 as filename OUFS.xls.

The OUFS, designed to be used in Excel, provides you with a spreadsheet template based on those used by professional analysts. The OUFS template is used to present the financial statistics for all the examples and case studies used in this block. A blank template is also provided on disk for you to use on future assignments and your own projects.

An analyst normally looks for something like a five-year history in order to establish trends in a company's performance. The reporting requirements in most jurisdictions ensure that the problem faced by analysts is not usually lack of information, but rather the need to select and focus on *relevant* information. By the end of this block you should have a system which will allow you to distil the relevant facts from this wealth of information in order to reach conclusions about a company from a variety of perspectives.

2.5   WHO IS THE ANALYST?

The priority for any user of an Annual Report is to decide what information will help answer the questions being posed. In order to do that, the user must be clear as to the question he or she is hoping to answer. For example, banks lending money to a company for a fixed period can restrict their analysis to the period during which the debt would be outstanding. They can limit their investigation to considering whether the company can meet its obligations to trading partners and other debt providers who rank equally as creditors. They may choose to ignore the question as to whether the company can generate profit for shareholders – although they should bear in mind that any company must provide a return to shareholders if it is to survive in the medium to long term!

By clarifying your objective, you can set aside information that has no bearing on the questions in hand and immediately simplify the analytic process.

Given that different users are asking different questions, they may also choose to define ratios in different ways. Many ratios have no universally accepted definition. For the purposes of this block we have used a series of ratios, calculated by the OUFS spreadsheet, using specific definitions considered in detail below and set out in the Software Guide. We have included a range of ratios that reflect the interests of most users and imposed common definitions so that ratios are comparable over time and across competitors. It is important to realise that other equally valid definitions are possible. Analysts calculate ratios that suit their analytic perspective or the conclusion they are hoping to reach. You should bear this in mind before interpreting ratios calculated by others, especially when those preparing the numbers have a vested interest in the outcome of the analytical exercise.

BOX 2.3   DIVIDEND COVER?

The 1996 Annual Report of Albert Fisher Group plc, an international food group processing and distributing fruit, vegetables and seafood, provides a good illustration of the use of carefully defined ratios.

On the basis of the UK's Financial Reporting Standard No. 3 'Reporting Financial Performance', which recommends the inclusion of both continuing and discontinuing activities, and non-operating exceptional items, the company reported the following dividend cover ratios during the previous five years:

	1992	1993	1994	1995	1996
Earnings per share (pence)	1.7	2.4	3.3	2.9	(17.1)
Net dividend per share (pence)	3.67	3.67	3.71	3.75	3.75
Dividend cover (times)	0.5	0.7	0.9	0.8	–

Dividend cover is calculated as

$$\frac{\text{Earnings per share}}{\text{Net dividend per share}}.$$

On the recommended definition, dividends were 'uncovered' (that is, dividend cover was less than one) throughout the period, with the company reporting a 17.1 pence loss per share in 1996. Nonetheless the following statements were included in the 1996 Chairman's Statement and in the report by the Finance Director for that year:

'The board recommends a maintained final dividend of 1.90 pence net per ordinary share. Together with the interim dividend of 1.85 pence net, this makes a total for the year of 3.75 pence net, the same as the previous year. This is covered 1.1 times by earnings per share before non-operating exceptional items.' (*Stephen Walls, Chairman's Statement*)

'The cash flow shows a net cash inflow from operating activities of £57 million, sufficient to cover dividend payments of £27 million and interest costs of £10 million.' (*Ian Quinlan, Finance Director, Financial Review*)

We examine Albert Fisher's performance in more detail in Sections 6 and 7.

Before we begin to consider the Annual Report, it is helpful to observe that almost all parties using the accounts are actually interested in the *future* performance of a company. Historical performance is interesting for the analyst only to the extent that it provides an insight into what is likely to happen in the future. Recognising this fact helps us to understand why some information is disregarded and other information is the focus of much attention.

2.6   USING RATIOS

In this unit you will become familiar with a range of ratios, calculated on the basis of information provided in an Annual Report, that can be used to evaluate the performance of a company. In using ratios to evaluate performance between companies it must be clearly recognised that comparisons are impacted upon by the underlying accounting rules adopted.

Before you can make any judgement on the basis of these ratios, you must consider the economic environment within which a company is operating. For example, sales growth of 10% may be acceptable when nominal GNP is growing at the same rate, impressive when nominal GNP is growing at 5%, and poor when nominal GNP is growing at a rate of 20%. As well as the general economic environment, you must take into account the industrial environment within which the company is operating. For example, in a declining industry it may be a creditable achievement to maintain the level of sales. In order to provide a basis for thinking systematically about the characteristics and prospects of the industry within which a company is operating, this unit will use the Porter 'five forces' model ('the Porter model'). Although the Porter model was originally devised as a framework for understanding and evaluating corporate strategy, it is widely used by financial institutions to provide the background for the ratio analysis of a company.

An analysis of the economy and sector within which a particular company operates will allow you to form an assessment of what is possible or normal. Ratio analysis of a company allows you to evaluate *what has been achieved* relative to what your analysis of the economic and industrial environment suggests is possible or normal.

The complex analytical task is simplified by dividing the analysis into four distinct phases, on the basis of a block of related ratios:

(i)   assessing the company's operating efficiency

(ii) assessing the company's financial structure

(iii) observing the consequences of the foregoing reflected in the company's profitability

(iv) evaluating the cash flows generated by the company relative to its cash obligations.

This analysis is based on accounting information. You may gain further insight into a listed company by considering market-related data as reflected in the final block of ratios included on the OUFS. (Unit 6 will go into more detail on these ratios when we look at valuing companies.)

In assessing the performance of a company on the basis of each block of ratios, you must consider three questions:

(i)   How have the ratios changed over time?

(ii) How do the ratios compare with those reported by similar companies?

(iii) Do the ratios make sense?

The first question, the performance of the company over time, is called **horizontal analysis**, **time series analysis** or **trend analysis**. As already mentioned, analysts typically look for a five-year history.

The second question, comparing performance with that reported by similar companies, is called **cross-sectional analysis**, **peer analysis** or **benchmarking**. Management may also wish to compare actual performance with budgeted performance.

The final question, whether the pattern of ratios makes sense, is the most challenging for novice analysts, but it is a question that can highlight serious problems. Indeed, it may be the only question you can ask if a company has a short history and there are no comparable companies.

Exercise 2.1

Blue Circle will be used as a case study throughout this course. Financial information from the Blue Circle Annual Reports for the years 1993–1996 has been entered in the OUFS input sheet found in Appendix 2. Using the 1997 Annual Report and the guidance in Appendix 3, enter the information still outstanding in the Assets, Liabilities, Income Statement and Division input sheets for 1997. The cells in which you need to enter information are indicated by a bold outline.

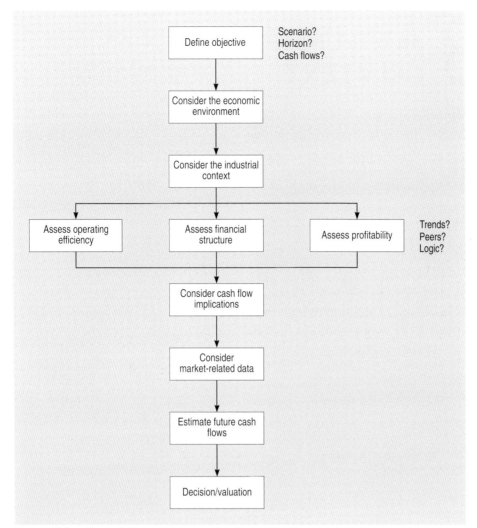

Figure 2.1 Financial analysis: a systematic approach

SUMMARY

In this section we considered why understanding the published Annual Report is an important skill. The logic of using the increasingly popular International Accounting Standards terminology and looking primarily at the Anglo-American accounting model was outlined. The contents of an Annual Report were summarised, and the importance of recognising the objective of the user of the accounts was reviewed. The OUFS, a spreadsheet template that allows you to put financial information into a standard form and automatically calculates a range of ratios on a consistent basis, was introduced. Finally, we set out the three questions that must be asked when interpreting financial ratios and introduced a flowchart that summarises a logical sequence that you may follow when sorting through the wealth of information available to you for assessing the performance of a company.

3 ANALYSIS IN CONTEXT

In this section we review the Porter 'five forces' model, which will be familiar to many of you. While not originally designed for the purpose, this model is widely used by financial institutions as a way of structuring the assessment of the sector which forms a background to the review of the financial ratios of a particular company in that sector. Other frameworks such as SWOT and STEEP analysis (see B800 *Foundations of Senior Management*) provide an alternative approach to understanding a sector. This section considers the application of the Porter model as a widely used approach that can provide considerable guidance to a novice analyst.

At the end of this section you should be able to:

*   summarise the Porter model
*   use the Porter model to structure the assessment of the potential profit in an industrial sector
*   apply the model to identify and evaluate the competitive strategy adopted by a company.

3.1 THE PORTER 'FIVE FORCES' MODEL

Some years ago, Michael Porter (1979) outlined a simple model to help companies formulate strategies to cope with the competitive situation they faced in their sector. Understanding what is possible in a sector gives you a useful guide as to what a company may achieve in the future.

Porter observes that potential profitability in a sector is determined by five factors:

(i)   the ease with which new entrants can join the sector

(ii)   the bargaining power of the sector's customers

(iii)   the bargaining power of the sector's suppliers

(iv)   the availability of alternative products and services which could meet the needs currently met by the sector's output

(v)   the behaviour of existing players in the sector.

Put simply, Porter suggests that the aggregate level of potential profits in a sector will depend on how easy it is for aspiring competitors to join the sector. The level of profits that remain within the sector will be influenced by the ability of suppliers or customers to capture a share of the potential profits through the price at which they do business with the sector. The price of substitute products and services which meet the same needs as the sector's products or services will act as a cap on the sector's prices and hence the industry's profit. Finally, Porter observes that the aggregate level of profits may be influenced by the behaviour of players within the sector; if there are a limited number of players it may be possible for them to act co-operatively to maximise the aggregate level of profit.

This simple model and Porter's elaboration of the factors which determine the strength of these five forces provide a checklist which can be used to help you think systematically about the profits which are possible in a sector. Those factors are described briefly below. The model has then been applied to two contrasting industries to illustrate how you can use the framework. A checklist briefly listing the key words cited in Porter's discussion of his model, and which can be a great help in structuring a strategic analysis, is included as Appendix 3.

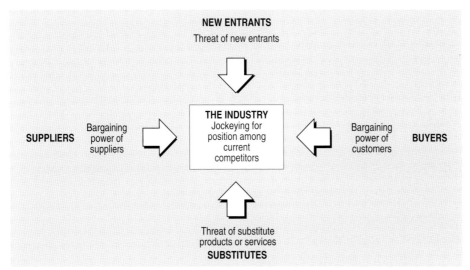

Figure 3.1   Forces governing competition in a sector. Reprinted by permission of *Harvard Business Review*. Exhibit from 'How competitive forces shape strategy', by Porter, M.E. March/April 1979. Copyright © 1979 by the President and Fellows of Harvard College. All rights reserved.

The threat of new entrants

The first factor to consider is the ease with which new entrants can join a sector. The harder it is for potential competitors to enter, the higher the returns that existing competitors will achieve.

Barriers to entry come in a variety of forms. Economies of scale can represent a considerable barrier since an aspiring entrant has to choose between coming in on a large scale or bearing a cost disadvantage. Certain technologies (such as a smelter requiring the maintenance of a furnace at a constant high temperature) carry scale economies in production. There are other key areas such as research, marketing, provision of after-sale service, distribution, utilisation of the sales force or financing, which may impose equally effective barriers. For example, if a sales force is to be fully occupied this can require relatively large-scale production. This may be a deterrent to entrants hoping to test the market with small-scale production unless they are willing to bear the disadvantages of non-specialist sales staff.

Product differentiation and brand identification can also create barriers since they mean that aspiring entrants must advertise and promote heavily in order to overcome customer loyalty. Soft drinks and over-the-counter drugs provide a good example of products differentiated through heavy advertising, but there are also examples such as merchant banking or accounting which are inherently difficult to evaluate but can be differentiated through track record or experience.

Capital requirements, be they for fixed assets, advertising, R&D, customer credit, inventories or absorbing start-up costs, may act as a barrier to aspiring entrants. The understandable preference which a lending bank has for the established large-scale producer may also provide an effective barrier to new entrants since the potential players would have to bear the expense of higher financing charges reflecting the financiers' greater perceived risk.

There may be cost disadvantages which are independent of size which block potential competitors: ownership of proprietary technology, access to raw material sources, assets purchased at pre-inflationary prices, government subsidies and favourable locations. Also, access to distribution channels can be an effective deterrent to new entrants. A potential entrant may have to match the scale and efficiency of existing competitors who may control the existing distribution network. It will be a particularly potent barrier when the company's products must reach end-users quickly because they involve an element of fashion (women's clothing), seasonality (fresh produce), or fad (children's toys).

Government policy can restrict entry to a market. Entry may be directly controlled through the requirement of licences (such as for the retailing of alcohol), the requirement for planning approval, or the need for health authority approval for human consumption. Entry may also be restricted indirectly by the imposition of health and safety, environmental or similar regulations.

Many regulated industries and public-sector industries are 'natural monopolies' because factors such as those listed above ensure that the first entrant or the largest entity will have an almost unbeatable cost advantage over others. The Porter model explains why policies such as the privatisation and breaking up of the electricity generators and distributors in the UK have been followed by re-consolidation across national boundaries and among different utilities as firms seek to achieve the economies of scale which will give them cost advantages relative to their competitors.

The bargaining power of customers

The bargaining power of customers will play a role in determining the level of profits since the more powerful customers are, the more likely they are to capture for themselves any potential profits.

A small number of potential customers creates the possibility of co-operative action to reduce prices. Similarly, large volume buyers may have great bargaining power; it will be particularly strong where fixed costs are high and manufacturers need to operate at full capacity.

If the product of the industry represents a significant element of customers' costs they are likely to direct a great deal of attention to that cost. Where the product is a minor element of customers' cost structures they are likely to be less price-sensitive.

If customers are operating in a sector characterised by low profits they are likely to direct attention towards cutting costs and therefore limiting the profits in the supplier sector.

If an input plays an important role in the perceived quality of the customer's output they are likely to be less price-sensitive. For example, a luxury car manufacturer could not accept anything but the highest quality materials for interior seating and trims; the end consumer would have little tolerance for any economies in this easily evaluated aspect of the product.

If a product saves the customer money he or she may be relatively price-insensitive. This may be observed in service areas such as merchant banking or auditing where poor advice may be embarrassing and expensive, so customers are willing to pay a premium to have the best advice available.

If customers are potential competitors, that is, if they could potentially manufacture the purchased inputs themselves or acquire their suppliers (actions termed 'backward integration'), prices and therefore profits will be kept in check.

The bargaining power of suppliers

Suppliers may also be in a position to capture a share of the potential profit of a sector.

If the supplier's sector has a small number of competitors, or at least fewer competitors than its customers, there may be scope for co-operative action that will keep input prices high and consequently reduce profits.

If the supplier's product is unique, differentiated in some way, or if there would be switching costs in moving to another supplier, they can charge a premium price, reducing potential profits in the customer's sector. If inputs can be readily substituted, the power of the supplier to erode profits will be kept in check.

The supplier may pose a threat of 'forward integration'. If this is the case, prices, and hence profits, are likely to be kept low to prevent forward integration happening.

Suppliers are more likely to price inputs aggressively if the sector is not an important customer, thereby limiting the customer's profits. If the supplier's future is linked to the customer's prosperity, aggressive pricing will be moderated.

The threat of substitute products or services

A supplier's ability to charge high prices will be curtailed if users can substitute another similar product for their output. There are obvious substitutes such as aluminium for steel, or sugar for honey, which limit the scope for charging a premium for either of the possible choices. There are also more indirect substitutes, including products and services which impose some switching costs (such as public transport and parking), which will none the less eventually limit the profits that can be made on either product.

The UK insurance industry provides a good example of the consequences of the emergence of a new substitute. High street insurance brokers have seen profits on personal insurance fall significantly with the emergence of direct telephone selling operations such as Direct Line and Churchill Insurance. In the face of competition provided through a new distribution network with lower costs, traditional brokers' prices and hence profits have declined markedly.

Jockeying for position

The behaviour of existing competitors in a sector can have a bearing on the aggregate level of profits which is achieved. If there are a small number of competitors it is possible that they may act co-operatively to maximise sector profits. If they do not act co-operatively, it is likely that the action that individual players take to maximise their own position by undercutting competitors will have the effect of reducing the overall level of profits.

Co-operative behaviour will be out of the question if there are a large number of competitors. Such behaviour is also unlikely in a situation where the market is growing slowly or declining, since individual players have a strong incentive to increase their rate of growth at the expense of other players. The lack of product differentiation or switching costs ensures that customers will respond very quickly to any player cutting prices.

If fixed costs represent a large component of total costs, every player will strive to work at full capacity, thereby encouraging competitive price cuts. Where capacity can only be increased in large increments, as through the building of a large factory, there are likely to be periods of over-capacity and consequent price-cutting.

High exit barriers can induce intense competition that reduces the overall level of profits in a sector. In recent years the UK has seen many retailers wishing to cut capacity but unable to sublet shops in a depressed property market. Many of them have discounted goods heavily in order to produce some contribution to a cost they are forced to bear.

Even if rivals are few in number, they are unlikely to act co-operatively if they are diverse in strategy, origin or personality. Richard Branson's high-profile cost cutting strategy for Virgin Airlines is the perfect example of a contrasting style and strategy undermining the co-operative behaviour previously observed in the airline industry.

3.2 COMPETITIVE STRATEGY

While facing the forces common to all participants within a sector, a company may choose to pursue one of three generic strategies. Porter proposes in a later book (1985) that, at the broadest level, these alternative strategic positions can be simply summarised as *cost leadership, differentiation* and *focus*. That is, a company can operate profitably in a given industry:

- by focusing on cost and seeking to become a low-cost, high-volume producer
- by focusing on product differentiation, often through advertising, and seeking high volume without price competition
- by focusing on a specialised market niche where it can provide a product tailored to a section of the market at a premium price.

These three generic strategies provide a very simple framework that underlines the need to choose a clear strategy in order to avoid being caught by the inherent contradictions among the strategies. For example, if the target market is a specific niche, efforts should focus on satisfying the needs of that niche in order to justify a premium price; cost cutting in order to build volume may introduce the risk of reducing quality and thus jeopardise both price and volume in the original niche. Similarly, if the objective is to be the lowest cost producer, then offering the embellishments provided by a competitor with a niche focus may simply increase costs without bringing compensatory price and volume increases.

This very simple framework provides a helpful starting point for analysing the factors that contribute to differing performances reported by companies within the same sector.

3.3 THE PORTER MODEL APPLIED – TWO EXAMPLES

The Porter 'five forces' model can be applied to any sector to help you think systematically about the characteristics of that sector and draw conclusions regarding the level of potential profits.

The application of the model to two contrasting sectors, UK high street fashion retailing and the manufacture and distribution of proprietary pharmaceuticals, is summarised in Tables 3.1 and 3.2 to illustrate how an analyst can use the model.

Table 3.1 UK high street fashion retailing	
FACTORS BUILDING PROFITS	**FACTORS LIMITING PROFITS**
Threat of new entrants	
• some economies of scale in advertising, design and distribution	• limited capital required to enter on a small scale with a single shop or market stall
• some brand identifications and loyalty but designs/styles easily copied, weakening any potential price advantage	• no government restrictions for national or international entrants
• prime locations are limited and can play an important role attracting customers	
• purchasing power	
Bargaining power of customers	
• many independent customers	• fashion is not a necessity
• clothing is a necessity	• many similar products and no switching cost
Bargaining power of suppliers	
• many fragmented suppliers	• there may be switching costs because timing of deliveries is crucial in the clothing industry (i.e. swim wear delivered in July may not be sold without discounting – the greater the 'fashion content' the more crucial the timing).
Threat of substitutes	
	• selling through mail order

Jockeying for position

- many players

- slow growth of market

- no switching costs

- high fixed costs for retailers in prime high street locations

- high exit barriers in depressed property market, given the long-term leases held by most high street retailers

Summary of competitive environment

To the extent that economies of scale operate, brand identity is established and the retailer has a prime location, profits may be enhanced.

However, any above-average profits are likely to be quickly eroded. There are many competitors who can readily copy the styles associated with any brand. Those competitors in prime locations face the pressure of high fixed costs (rent) and potential competitors can enter the market at very low costs (single shops or market stalls). This competitive pressure is heightened because it costs the customers nothing to change where they shop.

To the extent that retailers make profits, they are unlikely to have to share them with their customers or suppliers (there are too many to act collectively).

In consequence we would expect to see moderate profits which follow the economic cycle, reflecting the variation in customers' purchasing power and the actions of competitors seeking to cover high fixed costs during a recession.

Table 3.2 Manufacturing and distribution of proprietary pharmaceuticals	
FACTORS BUILDING PROFITS	**FACTORS LIMITING PROFITS**
Threat of new entrants	
• economies of scale in marketing, research and development, distribution and sales force	• expiry of patents
• product differentiation	
• huge start-up costs to research and develop a product and match economies of scale of existing players	
• drugs protected by patent laws with trade marks protecting other products	
• products often need government approval before being authorised for use	
Bargaining power of customers	
• highly differentiated, often unique products	• health authorities may purchase on behalf of many end-users
• products may be crucial to the customers' well being – they are unlikely to be price sensitive for products which may mean the difference between life and death	• health authorities may insist on the use of generic drugs

Bargaining power of suppliers

- research and development expertise may be unique

Threat of substitutes

- limited by government granted monopoly
- new discoveries

Jockeying for position

- few large players in each product area

- rapidly growing market given increasing standard of living and ageing population

Summary of competitive environment

Profits for established players with a portfolio of brands and patents are huge. The only significant threat comes from collective action by purchasing authorities.

This high level of profit is probably necessary to induce investors to accept the risk of developing a patentable drug, the possible cost of compensating customers for unforeseen side effects, and the possibility of finding their product superseded by a technically superior product.

Exercise 3.1 _____

Using the Porter checklist in Appendix 3, list the key factors which influence the maximum level of potential profits that could be achieved in the cement industry in the UK. The exercise provides a background for later exercises based on Blue Circle, a company that will be referred to throughout this course.

Before you begin this exercise, it may be helpful to note that cement is a bonding material widely used in the building industry. It is manufactured within narrow limits of chemical composition, so that it is a standard product all over the world. When combined with water, sand and gravel it hardens within a few hours to make the durable building material known as concrete.

Cement is manufactured through a series of processes. Limestone and clay or shale are quarried, then crushed to gravel size and stored separately. The two materials are dried, proportioned by weight, and ground to a fine powder called 'raw mix'. The blended mix is kiln-burned to partial fusion at 2700°F, when it forms glass-hard cement clinker. Gypsum is added and the mixture is ground to form Portland cement.

SUMMARY

In this section we reviewed the Porter 'five forces' model. We considered how the model may be used to understand the sector in which a company is operating and thus provide a background for more detailed analysis of an individual company's performance within that sector. The basic generic strategic options available to players within a sector were briefly reviewed. The insight that each of the five forces can provide regarding the potential profits in a sector was summarised, and the process was illustrated by applying the model to two contrasting sectors in the UK, high street fashion retailing and pharmaceuticals.

4 OPERATING EFFICIENCY

In this section we start the process of reviewing the ratios that allow us to evaluate the performance of a company by considering a company's **operating efficiency**. An efficient company in this context is one that chooses the appropriate pool of assets, and uses them in such a way that the maximum return is made to shareholders over time. In a not-for-profit organisation we would define efficiency as making the best use of an organisation's resouces in achieving its aims. This section will look at a number of ratios that measure the efficiency of a company at various stages within the cycle of production. At the end of this section you should be able to:

- outline the logic and standard definitions of operating efficiency or asset management ratios

- estimate the value of key operating efficiency ratios in a familiar industry

- suggest amendments to the standard definitions to reflect industry characteristics or accounting conventions.

4.1   THE CYCLE OF PRODUCTION

To provide a logical sequence to the discussion of the financial ratios relating to operating efficiency, we will review the cycle of production. The cycle of production, which can be applied to any sector, simply illustrates the process whereby cash is used to purchase inputs (raw materials), which are processed in some way (work in progress) to produce the company's output (finished goods). The finished goods are sold for cash, or create **accounts receivable** which are ultimately converted back to cash. By portraying the cycle in this simple way we can highlight the risks which the company may face at each stage of production. We can systematically calculate ratios that will alert us to any changes in the pattern of production relative to other players in the sector or within the company over time.

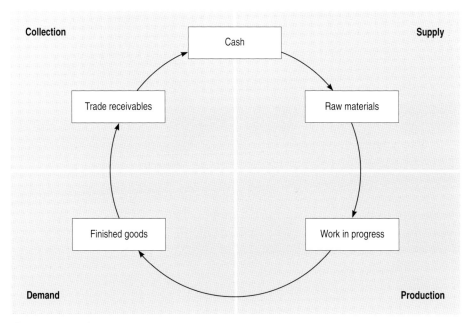

Figure 4.1   Operating efficiency: cycle of production

4.2   THE SUPPLY PHASE

The first stage of the cycle of production is the acquisition of raw materials. In order to come to a conclusion about the company's management of this stage of production, we can calculate ratios that will identify any changes in the pattern of holding or purchasing raw materials.

Raw material days

It is meaningless to look at the absolute level of raw materials that a company holds since we would expect these stocks to vary according to how much the company is producing. In order to make a meaningful comparison of raw material inventories over time and relative to competitors of different sizes, it is necessary to find a common denominator which will relate levels of raw materials on hand to the level of output. The common denominator is one day's worth of costs, which we estimate by dividing the reported annual cost of goods sold by 365. We then calculate the number of days of costs we hold in the form of raw materials by dividing the value of raw materials held by one day's worth of costs, that is:

$$\text{Raw material days} = \frac{\text{Raw material}}{\text{Cost of goods sold} \div 365}$$

$$= \frac{\text{Raw material} \times 365}{\text{Cost of goods sold}}$$

We are now in a position to judge whether the stores of raw material are rising relative to those of competitors or the company's performance in previous years.

It is crucial to recognise that while we need to identify any changes in the pattern of holding raw materials, we must do further analysis or investigation before we can conclude whether an observed movement is good or bad. Raw material days may rise because the company has not achieved the level of sales which it was expecting (a bad thing), because it has stockpiled a scarce resource (a good thing) or because it has introduced a new product line (a neutral thing).

BOX 4.1 A WARNING LIGHT

Ratios provide the 'warning lights' for analysts: the changes should always be investigated and interpreted. A change in any ratio, whether up or down, may indicate a positive development, a negative development or a change of no analytical significance.

It is also worth noting that we have a more useful indication of what is happening within the company when we focus on the components of inventory separately. The implications of an increase in raw materials can be very different from the increase in finished goods. If we focus only on the changes in total inventory we sacrifice a great deal of useful information.

Trade creditor days

While we are focusing on the supply stage of the cycle of production, we must also consider the payment terms that the company's suppliers are granting to them. This is an important ratio because a company's trading partners often know a great deal about the individual players in the industry they are supplying. Suppliers can be expected to shorten credit terms or insist on cash payments if they have doubts about a company's creditworthiness. On the other hand when a company is in severe difficulty and is not able to pay its suppliers this ratio will also rise. The ratio is calculated in a similar way to raw material days in that one day of costs is related to the level of trade creditors:

$$\text{Trade creditor days} = \frac{\text{Trade creditors} \times 365}{\text{Cost of goods sold}}$$

BOX 4.2 STOCK V. FLOW

The analyst must be very cautious when interpreting any ratio that includes figures from both the balance sheet and the income statement. The balance sheet is a 'snapshot' of a point in time or 'stock' while the income statement reflects a 'flow' over a period of time. This means that the assets included in the snapshot may not be those employed throughout the period reflected in the income statement.

If a company acquires a subsidiary just prior to the balance sheet date, the assets acquired will appear in the balance sheet but the revenues and expenses associated with the acquired subsidiary will be included in the income statement *only from the date of acquisition*. Everything else being equal, the inventory, trade creditors, accrued expenses and receivable days would increase, suggesting a deterioration in the efficiency with which the company is managing its net operating assets.

In reality, these movements in the ratios have no analytical significance and simply reflect the way we account for acquisitions and disposals.

4.3 THE PRODUCTION PHASE

We now move to the production phase of the cycle. In order to come to a conclusion about this stage of the cycle, we focus on the amount of inventory held in semi-processed form, the credit provided by suppliers of services used in production, the productivity of property, plant and equipment, the age of property plant and equipment and the rate at which it is being written off.

Work in progress days

Looking at the reported level of work in progress and using the same common denominator, we can calculate how many days of costs the company is holding as semi-finished goods.

$$\text{Work in progress days} = \frac{\text{Work in progress} \times 365}{\text{Cost of goods sold}}$$

Everything else being equal, the smaller the number of days, the more efficiently the raw materials are being processed. Again this generalisation should be made with caution, since a higher ratio (or 'slower' production cycle) may mean that goods are being produced to a higher specification or a lower ratio (or 'faster' production cycle) may simply reflect a changed product mix involving less complex products which may be manufactured more easily.

Accrued expenses days

The next area we focus on is the credit provided by those supplying services to the production process, of which labour forms the largest component. These services, received but not yet paid for, are included in the balance sheet as accrued expenses and once again we look at them relative to one day of costs:

$$\text{Accrued expenses days} = \frac{\text{Accrued expenses} \times 365}{\text{Cost of goods sold}}$$

Net property, plant and equipment turnover

There are a number of ratios relating to property, plant and equipment that are relevant to the production phase of the cycle. The most all-embracing is net property, plant and equipment turnover, which calculates the value of sales generated by each pound, dollar, etc. invested in property, plant and equipment:

$$\text{Net property, plant and equipment turnover} = \frac{\text{Sales}}{\text{Property, plant, equipment}}$$

In view of the way in which we account for assets, these ratios should be interpreted with great caution. Sales will reflect current market values. The assets, on the other hand, may be included in the balance sheet at a level substantially lower than market value. By focusing on property, plant and equipment turnover, we might make a comparison between two companies with identical machinery acquired at different times during a period of inflation. The ratio would indicate that the company with the older equipment – at the lower historical cost – appeared to be more efficient (i.e. generated more revenue for each pound invested in plant and equipment). The 'efficiency' will disappear when the equipment is eventually replaced at current market values.

BOX 4.3   HISTORICAL COST IN A PERIOD OF INFLATION

Difficulties arise in interpreting ratios that include long-term assets. You may have heard the old accounting professor's joke that he weighs three kilos, arguing that his weight at birth is as much a reflection of reality as the historic cost convention adopted in financial statements. Assets are generally included in the financial statements at the lower of historical cost or market value; in periods of inflation that will mean depreciated historical cost. The income statement, on the other hand, reflects flows which are close to current market prices. Any ratios combining the value of a long-term asset with current revenue and expenses will reflect currencies of very different vintages.

Great care must also be taken in inter-company comparisons, since what appear to be marked differences in the productivity of competitors, as measured by ratios such as net property, plant and equipment turnover, may simply reflect the fact that very similar assets were purchased several years apart during an inflationary period.

This distortion is one that must be kept firmly in mind when making comparisons between companies falling within different accounting models. Within the Franco-German model the revaluation of an asset normally gives rise to a liability for tax on the gain. In consequence assets are rarely revalued. Within the Anglo-American model, companies *may* revalue assets periodically (and generally do revalue property) in order to give a true and fair view of the company's position.

The article in Box 4.1 of Unit 1 illustrates this growing trend.

Plant life

In order to evaluate the company's management of the production phase of the cycle it may be useful to consider the age of plant and equipment and the rate at which they are being written off. Property is not normally included in these ratios as it is not likely to become technologically obsolete and is generally not depreciated.

Accepting the distortion that will result from inflation, the expected life of plant and equipment can be estimated by relating the historic cost of the asset to the depreciation charge for the year. The life used and the life remaining of assets can be estimated in a similar way:

$$\text{Expected life} = \frac{\text{Historic cost of plant and equipment}}{\text{Depreciation charge for year}}$$

$$\text{Life used} = \frac{\text{Accumulated depreciation of plant and equipment}}{\text{Depreciation charge for year}}$$

$$\text{Life remaining} = \frac{\text{Net book value of plant and equipment}}{\text{Depreciation charge for year}}$$

While these ratios are crude, they can serve the useful function of providing the analyst with a rough guide to the age of plant and equipment and any patterns of depreciation which are not in line with competitors. Ideally depreciation rates should reflect the economic life of an asset. In practice economic life may be hard to predict and governments often promote capital investment by allowing accelerated depreciation of assets. If depreciation is set at too high a rate, the company will hold assets worth more than the value included in the balance sheet and will therefore have 'hidden reserves'. If it is set at too low a rate the value of assets and profits will be overstated.

In view of the limitations of these plant and equipment-related ratios, they have not been included in the OUFS.

BOX 4.4   ACCELERATED CAPITAL CONSUMPTION ALLOWANCES?

Within the Franco-German model, accelerated capital consumption allowances (or depreciation of up to 100% in the year the asset is purchased) are routinely reflected in the company's accounts. This creates a hidden reserve in the form of fully written-down assets that do not appear on the balance sheet at all or assets that appear on the balance sheet at book values below their market value.

If an asset is fully written down (or written off) it has no remaining book value and there is nothing to appear on the balance sheet, although it is physically there – and playing a role in the production process – throughout its economic life.

It can pose a considerable challenge to define a single 'fair' value for an asset. Box 4.5 illustrates the complexity apparent when reviewing the range of accounting policies that must be used by a water company, whose assets include mains, sewers and reservoirs, as well as landfill sites, in addition to the more conventional land, buildings, vehicles, plant and equipment. Given this complexity, comparisons with other industries or companies reporting under different accounting standards must be made with extreme caution.

BOX 4.5   THAMES WATER PLC, ANNUAL REPORT AND ACCOUNTS 1996

The following extract illustrates the complexity of assigning a monetary value to assets such as nineteenth-century pipelines and landfill sites.

Principal accounting policies

[...]

Tangible fixed assets comprise:

- Infrastructure assets (being mains and sewers, impounding and pumped raw water storage reservoirs and sludge pipelines);
- Landfill sites; and
- Other assets (including properties, overground plant and equipment).

(i) **Infrastructure assets** comprise a network of systems. Expenditure on infrastructure assets relating to increases in capacity or enhancements of the network is treated as additions. Expenditure on maintaining the operating capability of the network in accordance with defined standards of service is charged as an operating cost and is classified as infrastructure renewals expenditure.

(ii) **Landfill sites** are included at cost less accumulated depreciation. The provision for depreciation is based upon the average cost per cubic metre of void space consumed from the deposit of waste. Provision is made for site restoration where it is anticipated that expenditure will be required at the end of the life of the site.

(iii) **Other assets** are included at cost less accumulated depreciation.

4.4   THE DEMAND AND COLLECTION PHASES

The next phases of the cycle of production are the demand phase and, if customers are granted credit terms, the collection phase. In order to evaluate the management of these stages of production we should look for changes in the pattern of holding finished goods or the terms on which they are sold.

Finished goods days

During this phase the company holds finished goods ready for sale. We again focus on the number of days of costs held as finished goods:

$$\text{Finished goods days} = \frac{\text{Finished goods} \times 365}{\text{Cost of goods sold}}$$

A rise in this ratio can be a sensitive indicator of sales that were expected but have not materialised. On the other hand, the build-up of goods prior to a major sales campaign would also cause this ratio to increase.

> ### BOX 4.6   COST OF GOODS SOLD IS NOT DISCLOSED?
>
> One day's worth of costs is the 'common denominator' that is conventionally used to calculate the 'days' ratios for those operating assets and liabilities that are included in the balance sheet at cost (that is inventory, trade creditors, accrued expenses and prepaid expenses). Accounts receivable days are calculated relative to a day's sales rather than a day's costs, as receivables reflect the sale price of goods sold (including any mark-up) rather than the cost price.
>
> When ratios include operating assets and liabilities which are included in the balance sheet at sale price, ratios are normally calculated relative to sales.
>
> Where the cost of goods sold is not available, all the days ratios may also be quoted relative to sales. This may be the case when accounts are prepared following the Franco-German model. Within the Franco-German model the income statement may focus on production, or total costs for the year, rather than sales for the year. This is discussed in greater detail in Section 6. If accounts are prepared on this basis, sales for the year will be disclosed but the cost of the goods *sold* will not be separated from total costs (that is, including the cost of additions to inventory).
>
> Calculating the days ratios on the basis of sales will highlight any changes within a company over time with equal effect, but users must make sure that they are comparing like with like when making any inter-company comparisons.

Receivable days

The production cycle is not complete until cash has been received, so the collection phase represents the final phase in the cycle for companies providing their customers with credit terms. Deferring payment is an important marketing tool in many industries. Analysts need to look for any changes in the company's credit policy or collection experience. A change in credit policy or a lengthening of collection times can be seen in the ratio of receivables to sales. This is usually expressed as receivable days calculated as the number of days of sales held as receivables:

$$\text{Receivable days} = \frac{\text{Receivables} \times 365}{\text{Sales}}$$

Exercise 4.1

Laura Ashley plc is a 'lifestyle' fashion clothing and home furnishings retailing group, operating a chain of retail shops in the UK, USA, Europe and East Asia. The group has had a disappointing record during the mid-1990s. The following figures were taken from the 1997 Annual Report:

Laura Ashley plc	27 Jan. 1996 £m	25 Jan. 1997 £m
Sales	336.6	327.6
Cost of goods sold	172.0	168.9
Trade debtors	7.6	11.1
Creditors	28.5	41.3
Accrued expenses	11.8	15.7

Using the figures listed above, and your understanding of the retail industry, estimate the level of inventory you would expect to see on the balance sheet at 25 January 1997. You may find it helpful to review Table 3.1, 'UK high street fashion retailing' in Section 3.3.

4.5 NET OPERATING ASSETS

While focusing on the production cycle we can see that a part of the company's funding arises directly from the cycle of production through the credit terms offered by the company's suppliers. This source of funding is very attractive. Providing the company pays suppliers at the time agreed and so is not subject to any penalties, such funding is essentially free. A key element in the management of the production cycle, therefore, is the management of the relationship with suppliers of both goods and services.

A company's costs will be minimised if it holds a minimum level of inventory, collects revenue from customers as quickly as possible and pays suppliers as slowly as possible. The measure that focuses on this aspect of a company's management is net operating assets. Net operating assets are calculated as the difference between the assets directly related to the cycle of production (inventories held plus receivables due from customers) less the liabilities directly related to the cycle of production (the credit granted by suppliers, including the work force and other suppliers of services):

Accounts receivable

+ Inventory

+ Prepaid expenses

– Trade creditors

– Accrued expenses

= Net operating assets

Net operating assets are not the same as the more broadly defined working capital (current assets less current liabilities) which will be discussed in Section 5.2. Net operating assets restricts focus to the assets and liabilities connected directly with the cycle of production, and provides a sensitive measurement of the efficiency of the company's management of the cycle.

Net operating assets could equally well be expressed over cost of goods sold, but that is not what analysts do. You will see all these overall ratios measured relative to sales by brokers, etc.

To be comparable across companies or over time, net operating assets must be related to the level of output. Thus a key measurement of the company's efficiency in the management of those things it can influence in the short term through its management of the production cycle is net operating assets/sales, which is normally expressed as a percentage.

4.6   SERVICE ORGANISATIONS

We have used a cycle of production typical in a manufacturing company to provide a logical sequence for our discussion of the ratios relating to operating efficiency. The cycle of production in a service organisation may be illustrated as a shortened cycle in which the manufacturing or production phase disappears. While the ratios relating to the efficiency of the production phase are not relevant to the service sector, those ratios relating to the supply, demand and collection phases remain of interest.

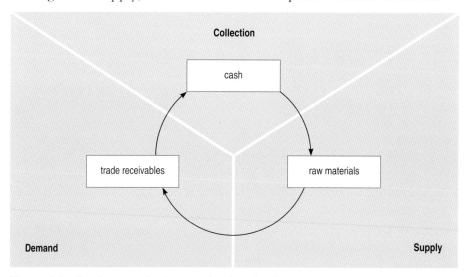

Figure 4.2   Service organisations: cycle of production

A very wide range of organisations may be described as service industries and they may, or may not, require investment in fixed assets. This is characteristic of many public sector and not-for-profit organisations. Organisations, such as insurance brokers, commodity dealers or retailers, purchase goods and services that they sell on at a higher price than they have paid because of their greater knowledge or because they have repackaged the product. Some, such as advertising agencies or firms of solicitors, purchase manpower skills that they can sell on to end-users at a premium. Others, such as hotels or health clubs, own fixed assets, the use of which they offer to end-users.

The operating efficiency ratios relating to the supply, demand and collection phases in a service industry apply in much the same way as they do for manufacturers. For example, an advertising agency that collects receivables promptly and maximises finance available from suppliers such as providers of media space will produce a higher return for shareholders than an equally creative agency that is lax in these areas.

Measures focusing on the efficiency in the use of fixed assets in a service industry are often specific to that industry. Instead of the manufacturers' net property, plant and equipment turnover, we may look at ratios such as occupancy rates (hotels) or sales per square foot (retailers).

'Clearly, someone is not holding up his end.'

The returns to shareholders in service industries are often linked primarily to the skills and knowledge of the employees of the company. As these do not appear on the balance sheet, we see only indirect evidence of the efficiency with which skills and knowledge are employed in the level of sales achieved and the operating profits retained on those sales.

Exercise 4.2

Table 4.1 shows the operating efficiency ratios for Blue Circle for the years 1993–1996. Using the input sheets you completed in Exercise 2.2, calculate the same ratios for 1997.

Is the mix of assets held by Blue Circle what you would expect to find in this industry?

Look at Blue Circle's policy on asset valuation, which can be found in the 'Accounting Policies' section (page 42) of the 1997 Annual Report. Does this policy influence your assessment of the efficiency of Blue Circle's asset management on the basis of these ratios?

Table 4.1 Blue Circle operating efficiency ratios						
Operating efficiency	OUFS line ref.	30.12.93	30.12.94	30.12.95	31.12 .96	31.12.97
Trade creditor days	218*287/313	38.78	39.70	43.23	40.67	36.49 ✓
Accrued expenses days	219*287/313	40.30	46.83	45.91	43.32	40.12 ✓
Inventory days	125*287/313	75.48	71.07	84.51	76.44	80.13 ✓
– Raw material days	119*287/313	26.37	26.49	32.19	32.60	36.89 ✓
– Work in progress days	120*287/313	15.30	10.79	15.27	14.54	11.24 ✓
– Finished goods days	121*287/313	33.80	30.79	37.04	29.30	32.00 ✓
Trade receivable days	117*287/312	63.05	61.15	61.21	55.77	59.66 ✓
Net operating assets (£m)	117+125+136–218–219	301	273	307	267	349. ✓
Net operating assets/sales	426/312	17.92	15.33	17.29	14.71	18% ✓
Net property, plant and equipment turnover	312/148	1.64	1.81	1.78	1.88	1.59. ✓

SUMMARY

In this section we reviewed a range of ratios that provide a picture of how efficiently a company is managing each stage of its cycle of production. Overall efficiency measures such as net operating asset/sales percentage or net property, plant and equipment turnover were also introduced. The application of these operating efficiency measures to service industries, where organisations may own very few fixed assets, was summarised.

Having considered how efficiently a company has managed its assets, we now turn to the measures that allow us to evaluate how a company has financed its investment in assets.

5 FINANCIAL STRUCTURE

After assessing the company's operating efficiency, we turn to an examination of how the company has chosen to finance its activities. A company may have a good record of operating efficiency but fail because the activities are inappropriately financed.

In this section we consider the measures that assess the availability of finance for a company's activities in the short term, known as **liquidity ratios**, and measures that assess the stability of finance in the longer term – **solvency ratios**.

At the end of this section you should be able to:

- outline the logic and standard definitions of liquidity ratios and solvency ratios

- suggest amendments to the standard definitions to reflect sector characteristics or accounting conventions

- appreciate the limitations of liquidity and solvency ratios.

5.1 SOURCES OF FINANCE

Figure 5.1 (overleaf) shows a graphical representation of a simple balance sheet with the size of each category in proportion to the category's monetary value. The unshaded categories indicate those sections of the balance sheet which reflect operating decisions, and the shaded area indicates those sections of the balance sheet which reflect financing decisions. As the diagram graphically illustrates, the company's operating decisions will determine the scale of the unshaded categories and consequently how much non-operational finance is required in order to make the balance sheet balance.

Given the overall amount of finance needed, the management's task is to choose the kind needed (that is, debt, equity or other creditors), and its maturity, in order to ensure that they are never paying for funding which they do not require (flexibility), that the funding which is needed is always available (stability) and that the cost of funding is minimised.

Remember the distinction between debt, which is a liability, and debtors, which are assets.

Debt and equity represent the potential sources of finance external to the company. Trade credit and accrued expenses arising from the cycle of production, and equity arising through the retention of the profits of past cycles of production together represent the internal sources of finance.

Before considering the optimum balance between debt and equity that should be raised, it is helpful to compare some of the characteristics of these two possible sources of finance.

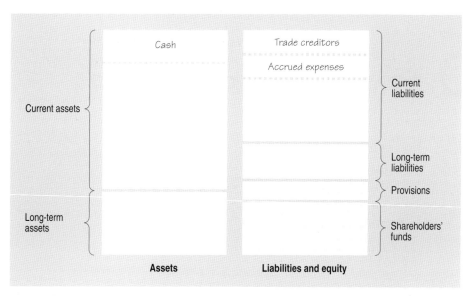

Figure 5.1   The balance sheet. Shaded areas reflect financing decisions.

- Debt and equity differ in the obligation that they carry for repayment. Debt is generally repayable on a specific date or series of dates. Equity generally carries no obligation for repayment by a company.

- The actual amount of, or the formula for determining, the annual cash payment (or interest) to debt providers is determined by a legally enforceable contract. The annual cash payment (dividends) to providers of equity is at the discretion of the board of directors.

- In the event of a liquidation, unsecured debt will rank equally with unsecured creditors for repayment from the proceeds of the liquidation. Equity has only residual rights in a liquidation and therefore receives a share of the liquidation proceeds only after all unsecured creditors have been fully repaid.

Remember uncertainty of income risk from Unit 1.

- Since the uncertainty of both the timing and level of payment for equity means that it carries a greater risk to the providers of this type of finance than debt, it offers a greater expected return to the investors and represents a greater expected cost to the company than does debt.

The management's objective of maximising shareholder value, discussed in Unit 1, implies an objective of minimising financing costs. Long-term debt is often more expensive than short-term debt (as we shall see in Block 3), and so one way of minimising costs and ensuring complete flexibility would be for management to fund all activity through short-term debt. Few actually choose this course. If a company is funded exclusively through short-term debt (which is normally repayable on demand), there is no assurance that the funds will remain available throughout the period during which they are required. If funding is withdrawn, and cannot be replaced, the company will go out of business.

So, in order to ensure that funding is available for long-term investments, a company tries to match the maturity of the finance instrument with the life of the investment being financed. This is particularly true of project finance, where the finance is linked specifically to a particular project.

Debt is the only instrument available to match a short-term or temporary (seasonal) financing need but either debt or equity could be chosen to meet long-term financing needs.

Equity offers the possibility of a higher rate of return to funds providers than debt and hence is more expensive as a source of finance. While more expensive than debt, equity has the advantage of allowing much more flexibility in timing of the providers' required returns. Debt, though cheaper, requires servicing on a fixed schedule or the enterprise may go out of business. The greater the uncertainty or variability of an enterprise's performance, therefore, the more it should use equity finance.

To summarise, managers need to check that they are not paying for financing which they do not need, while ensuring that the financing they do need is there for as long as it is required at the minimum cost. In order to achieve this, managers should match the period for which the asset is held to the period for which funding is assured (matching the economic lives of the assets to the maturity of finance). With respect to long-term assets, managers should also ensure an appropriate split between debt (which must be serviced regularly) and equity (which requires a greater return but allows greater flexibility in the timing of those returns). This split between equity and debt is referred to as a company's capital structure and this will be the subject of Unit 4. We now go back to short-term finance decisions.

5.2 LIQUIDITY

The first financing issue is whether the company can meet its liabilities as they fall due within the coming year. It is a key focus because an organisation that is unable to make payments as they fall due will cease to trade. There are three measures that can be used to determine how 'liquid' a company is, although all have certain limitations.

Current ratio

The current ratio looks at the level of current assets relative to the level of current liabilities:

$$\text{Current ratio} = \frac{\text{Current assets}}{\text{Current liabilities}}$$

This ratio assumes that the current assets can be converted to cash at book value to meet the liabilities that are falling due within the year. The ratio carries two implicit assumptions that are unlikely to be met.

(i) Creditors will be satisfied by payment within the year when in practice they will focus on a specific due date which may be much more immediate.

(ii) Current assets will realise their book value; this may be true of some assets such as cash or trade receivables but it is not likely to be true of others such as the semi-finished goods held as work in progress, or for pre-paid expenses.

Accepting these implicit assumptions for a moment, it is worth contemplating what the ratio implies. Logic would lead to the conclusion that if the ratio is equal to or greater than 1.0, the company will have no liquidity crisis in the year. Consider now the situation in which the management has bargaining strength *vis à vis* both customers and suppliers; they can call for immediate payment from customers, but defer payment to suppliers – which they should do if they are to minimise costs and maximise profits. The effect of efficiently managing the relationship with both customers and suppliers may well be to make the current ratio less than 1.0. Provided that, if the company is a going concern, we expect the liabilities arising during the year to be met through trading revenues rather than through liquidation of the assets, we should not be concerned if the current ratio is less than 1.0.

Quick (acid test) ratio

Uncertainty about the value of current assets is addressed by the quick ratio (also called the 'acid test') which looks only at those current assets most readily convertible to cash:

$$\text{Quick ratio} = \frac{\text{Current assets} - \text{Inventory}}{\text{Current liabilities}}$$

While this ratio makes the very conservative assumption that inventory will generate no cash and the brave assumption that all accounts receivable can be collected, it does not address the other limitation of the current ratio outlined above.

Working capital

It is also helpful to look at interest cover as a measure of liquidity. This is covered in Section 6.2.

The final measure that is calculated to estimate a company's liquidity is working capital:

Working capital = Current assets – Current liabilities

This is an estimate of the size of liquidity in monetary terms rather than a ratio but it has the same limitations as the current ratio as a measure of liquidity.

All these measures are widely used to assess liquidity, but the cash flow ratios (which we consider in Section 8) actually do a better job of answering the underlying question of whether the company can meet the liabilities falling due within the next year.

Exercise 5.1

In 1995 Tesco plc and J. Sainsbury plc, both large UK food retailers, reported the following:

	Tesco plc 25 Feb 1995 (£m)		J. Sainsbury plc 9 Mar 1995 (£m)	
Turnover		10,101	Turnover	11,357
Cost of goods sold		(9,298)	Cost of goods sold	(10,241)
Cash in hand and at banks		44	Cash in hand and at banks	199
16.29 Inventory		415	Inventory	509 *19 14*
Trade receivables *3.76*		104	Trade receivables *5.62*	172
Investments		131	Investments	2
Total current assets		**694**	**Total current assets**	**882**
Short-term debt		298	Short-term debt	231
29.38 Trade creditors		723	Trade creditors	725 *25.94*
45¹ Accrued expenses		115	Accrued expenses	95 *3.39*
Other current liabilities*		645	Other current liabilities*	785
Total current liabilities		**1,781**	**Total current liabilities**	**1,836**
Net operating assets		(319)	Net operating assets	(139)
Current ratio		0.39	Current ratio	0.48

Net operating assets is inventory plus trade receivables, less trade creditors and accrued expenses.

* These sums include other creditors, taxes payable, leases and dividends payable

In both companies, net operating assets were negative and the current ratio was well below 1.0.

What are the implications of this lack of liquidity?

Which company has the stronger performance in terms of operating efficiency? Use ratios to justify your answer.

5.3 SOLVENCY

Moving our horizon from the short to the long term we can now consider the company's ability to meet long-term liabilities as and when they fall due for payment, known as its **solvency**.

Before we look at the ratios that focus on solvency it is important to remind ourselves that long-term debt or equity can provide relatively long-term funding. Long-term debt is generally cheaper than equity, particularly for a tax-paying organisation, but it brings with it the requirement to make interest payments and principal repayments at set times. Equity, while requiring a greater return to compensate for the greater risk of its junior status in a liquidation, carries no obligation to provide returns at a set time. In consequence, the greater the variability in a company's performance the more the requirement for long-term finance should be met through equity rather than debt; that is, the riskier the business the greater the dependence on equity rather than debt. Also, access to equity markets may be a realistic option only for fairly large firms, with established records. Public-sector organisations, by their very nature, do not have access to equity.

Some nationalised industries have, however, issued 'quasi-equity' – that is debt with some equity characteristics.

There are several variations of solvency ratios that we routinely calculate, some including the broadest definitions of liabilities (such as contingent liabilities) and some including only liabilities relating to debt. Some solvency ratios make very conservative assumptions about the value of intangible assets, some recognise their full book value. The choice of solvency ratio depends upon the characteristics of the sector and scenario (that is, 'worst case', 'most likely case', etc.) of interest to the analyst. A range of solvency ratios is automatically calculated by the OUFS, but only one or two ratios will best reflect the characteristics of the sector and the perspective of the analyst.

Senior creditors, such as employees, suppliers and lenders, can think of the shareholders as providing an 'equity cushion'. In a liquidation, senior creditors' claims are met in full before any funds are paid to shareholders. Consequently, the liquidation proceeds of the assets of a company must fall below the book value of the assets by an amount greater than shareholders' funds before senior creditors are not able to be repaid in full. So, from the senior creditors' point of view, shareholders' funds represent a 'cushion' against losses in the event of a liquidation, and the greater the proportion of shareholders' funds relative to total assets, the greater the cushion provided.

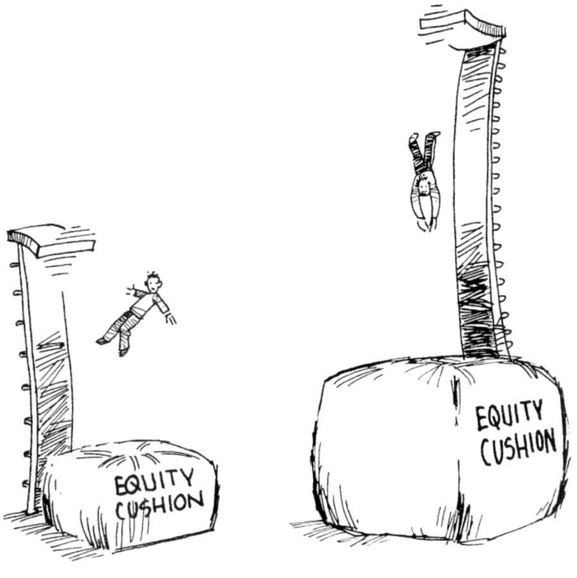

Although a range of solvency ratios can be calculated, the two most commonly used are **gearing** and the debt/equity ratio. We will look at these first.

Gearing

The first solvency ratio we shall consider focuses on the relative dependence on debt and equity, and is called gearing:

$$\text{Gearing \%} = \frac{\text{Short- and long-term debt}}{\text{Equity}} \times 100$$

The more uncertain the level of cash generated by a company's operations, the more it should depend on equity and hence the lower the level of gearing that will be consistent with long-term survival.

Once you have calculated gearing, you might consider how the number should be judged. Comparisons with others in the sector, analysis of that sector, and comparisons with gearing ratios in other sectors that you consider more or less risky, can help you to judge whether the balance between debt and equity is appropriate.

Debt/equity ratio

An alternative ratio that is often used to assess the relative dependence on debt and equity is the debt/equity ratio. A wide variety of definitions are used; they may all share the same name, but they may include both long- and short-term debt in their numerator, and equity, or equity plus debt, in their denominator; the equity may also be valued on an accounting or a market basis. All these alternative definitions give a picture of the relative dependence on debt and equity – you must simply make certain that comparisons over time or between companies are calculated on a consistent basis. The OUFS calculates the debt/equity ratio on the basis of the book value of shareholders' equity as follows:

$$\text{Debt/equity ratio} = \frac{\text{Short- and long-term debt}}{\text{Short- and long-term debt} + \text{Shareholders' equity}}$$

Although gearing and the debt/equity ratio are the most commonly used measures of solvency, you may well encounter a range of other ratios tailored for specific sectors and perspectives. Examples of some of these are given below.

Net gearing

A refinement of the gearing ratio that analysts often use is net gearing. On the assumption that cash and marketable securities do not play a role in the cycle of production, they could be immediately available to repay debt. Net gearing shows debt less cash and marketable securities to give a clearer picture of the relative dependence on debt and equity:

$$\text{Net gearing \%} = \frac{\text{Short- and long-term debt} - \text{Cash and marketable securities}}{\text{Equity}} \times 100$$

The validity of looking at net rather than gross gearing depends on whether the cash and marketable securities are in fact available to extinguish debt. They could be invested overseas and inaccessible (consider Polly Peck, a company whose assets in Northern Cyprus were outside the jurisdiction of the UK courts and thus unavailable to creditors following the company's liquidation) or they could be required as a means of exchange for the cycle of production (i.e. balances in the tills of a retailer), so this adjustment is not always justifiable.

Leverage ratios

Given that other creditors rank equally with debt and require timely servicing, it can be argued that looking only at debt may inappropriately underestimate the dependence on 'debt-like' funding. The leverage ratio reflects this broader view and looks at all long-term liabilities relative to equity:

$$\text{Leverage} = \frac{\text{Long-term liabilities}}{\text{Equity}}$$

Analysts (such as lenders) interested in a 'worst case' situation may need to make further adjustments to the leverage ratio. Intangibles are often seen as the least liquid assets; moreover, the value at which intangibles are included in the balance sheet shows little consistency even within a single jurisdiction. In consequence, analysts interested in the worst case situation routinely make the implicit assumption that intangibles have no market value and reduce the shareholders' equity accordingly:

$$\text{Leverage (tangible)} = \frac{\text{Total liabilities}}{\text{Equity} - \text{Intangible assets}}$$

Intangibles can be intellectual property such as publishing rights, brand names and patents, or they can be goodwill arising on consolidation. In the case of goodwill, the conservative assumption that the market value in liquidation is zero may be justifiable. Intellectual property (for example, the publishing rights to Lennon–McCartney songs) may have a readily identified and realisable market value. Leverage (tangible) may be the appropriate focus, but care should be taken to recognise the precise nature of the intangibles or real economic value may be overlooked.

You may also need to consider contingent liabilities. Contingent liabilities are those liabilities which may emerge in certain circumstances but are not yet listed in the balance sheet and would rank equally with other long-term liabilities in a liquidation:

$$\text{Leverage (incl. contingents)} = \frac{\text{Total liabilities} + \text{Contingent liabilities}}{\text{Equity} - \text{Intangible assets}}$$

Such liabilities that the directors and auditors conclude are material may have to be disclosed in the notes to the accounts. It is important to recognise that it is not equally likely that all contingent liabilities will be crystallised; the likelihood that they will occur may range from probable to remote. For example, payments under a guarantee provided to the creditors of a troubled former subsidiary may have a reasonably high probability of being realised, while recourse on high-quality receivables discounted by bankers has a low probability of being realised. As an analyst, you should assess the disclosed contingent liabilities with care as they can be very large relative to an organisation's resources.

You must also consider possible future liabilities that the directors and auditors have *not* disclosed as contingent liabilities in the notes to the accounts (because they judge that they are remote possibilities).

BOX 5.1   SEARS PLC

The 1997 Annual Report and Accounts of Sears plc provides two good examples of the scale of liabilities that can emerge while not being included as contingent liabilities because it was judged that the possibility of their crystallisation was remote.

In order to dispose of a number of troubled shoe businesses, in 1995–96 Sears sold their trademarks, fixtures and fittings and stock to Facia Ltd and negotiated an option for the sale of the related trading properties. The property sale was treated in the accounts as if it had happened, since contracts had been exchanged. By May 1996, Facia's financial condition had deteriorated sufficiently to require it to be put into administration. The options relating to the sale of the properties could not be exercised and Sears had to make a provision of £32.5m relating to the subsequent disposal of these properties. Sears included no contingent liability or other disclosure in the 1996 accounts owing to the remote possibility that the put option could not be exercised.

The Sears accounts for 1997 also outline a possible liability resulting from a possible action by the Inland Revenue, which (at the time of writing) has filed a legal appeal regarding the tax treatment of the disposal of a business in 1988. On the basis of advice from tax counsel regarding the low chance of the case succeeding, no contingent liability has been included in the accounts. If the case does succeed the liability would be £80 million plus interest (the operating profit for 1996–7 was £88.9m).

Capital employed

A further approach to assessing the stability of funding is to calculate the total long-term funds used by the company. Long-term debt, long-term liabilities, long-term provisions and equity provide obvious sources of long-term funding, but a further source is provided by the short-term debt which remains on the balance sheet at year-end. The sum of these sources of long-term funds is termed capital employed:

Short-term debt

+ Long-term debt

+ Long-term liabilities

+ Long-term provisions

+ Shareholders' equity

= Capital employed

Long-term funding, measured as capital employed, may be compared to the level of external claims against the company through the ratio:

$$\frac{\text{Total liabilities}}{\text{Capital employed}}$$

As we observed in our discussion of asset valuation, the book value of an asset may be very different from its market value or replacement cost. All the foregoing solvency ratios are based on the book value of equity, and consequently reflect the company's asset valuation policy. If the book value of an asset is below the market value, investors may recognise this 'hidden value' by increasing the price they are willing to pay for the company's shares. For this and other reasons, the market value of shares may be very different from their book value. The market value of shareholders' equity (or market capitalisation) is calculated by multiplying the current share price by the number of shares issued and outstanding. The market capitalisation of shares may be viewed as the consensus view of the market value of a company's assets and consequently provides a useful estimate of the 'real' value of shareholders' equity. By comparing the market capitalisation of a firm to the level of its debt, you have a refinement of the earlier solvency measures which were based on book values and thus a useful estimate of the true equity cushion. It is also the measure of equity value we will need when looking at a company's capital structure and cost of capital in Unit 4.

This, and other market-related measures, are discussed in Section 6.4.

BOX 5.2 TO REVALUE OR NOT TO REVALUE?

Within the Anglo-American bloc, fixed assets such as land and buildings are normally revalued to reflect current market prices. The effect of these revaluations is to increase the revaluation reserve and hence the book value of shareholders' equity. Gearing and leverage therefore fall following a revaluation.

Within the Franco-German bloc assets are generally not revalued as it would give rise to a liability for tax on the gain.

In consequence, gearing and leverage appear higher within the Franco-German bloc and comparisons with companies outside the bloc should be made with caution.

Seasonal debt

We pointed out in Section 4 that the year-end balance sheet normally represents the low point in the company's seasonal cycle. The level of debt and hence the debt/equity ratio at other points during the year may be very much higher.

While the high point debt/equity ratio is not often available to analysts, an indication of the existence of a seasonal pattern is provided by comparing the ratio of annual interest expense to the average level of year-end debt with market rates of interest. The scale of the difference provides a rough and ready guide to the degree of seasonality.

$$\text{Interest expense/Average debt} = \frac{\text{Interest expense year}_1}{(\text{Debt year}_0 + \text{Debt year}_1) \div 2}$$

Consider the balance sheet of a toy company in October when they are likely to be holding a high proportion of the year's anticipated sales as pre-Christmas inventory and the balance sheet of the same company in January after the inventory has been sold.

Gearing = 206.1% ✓

D/E Ratio = 0.67 ✓

Net Gearing = 201.6% ✓

Leverage = 2.99 ✓

Lev (Tan) = -2.08 ✓

Leverage (Inc Cont) = -2.08 ✓

CE = 3,373

TL/CE = 0.74

Exercise 5.2

Calculate the solvency ratios for Maxwell Communication Corporation plc at year-end 1991, using the data below. Which ratios should have provided a warning of the risk posed by the group which went into liquidation shortly after this balance sheet date?

	£m
Debt	1,788.6
Total liabilities	2,505.3
Shareholders' equity	867.7
Intangible assets	2,069.4
Contingent liabilities	6.2
Cash	39.0

SUMMARY

In this section we reviewed the various ratios that can assess how a company has chosen to finance its activities. Immediate prospects are assessed by looking at the company's liquidity, or its ability to meet claims falling due from the proceeds of short-term assets. Longer-term financial stability can be assessed by looking at measures of solvency or the ability to meet longer-term claims as they fall due. The caution that should be exercised in interpreting these ratios was underlined by considering the range of possible accounting and market values of assets (and thus shareholders' equity), debt and contingent liabilities.

The liquidity and solvency ratios focus on what cash can be realised by selling assets. It may be more meaningful to consider the cash that can be realised by the company as a going concern, since payments will be met from operating revenues, not liquidation proceeds, if the company continues to trade. If we wish to know whether the company can meet its obligations as they fall due in the short term (liquidity) or the medium term (solvency) it is often more useful to focus on the company's ability to generate cash through its operating activities, or its cash flow, as we will see in Section 8.

6 PROFITABILITY

This section considers the element of financial statements that summarises the consequences of the operating and financing decisions taken by management – the income statement. We consider the structure of the income statement and the definitions of the conventional **profitability ratios**. We also consider the difference between core and non-core income, an important distinction when we need to forecast future performance. A range of ratios that relate profitability to share price will be reviewed. The final sub-section considers how similar performance ratios might be calculated when profit is not the objective of the organisation.

By the end of this section you should be able to:

- outline the logic and standard definitions of profitability ratios
- define conventional share price ratios
- outline the principles that could be used to define ratios to help assess output and outcomes in not-for-profit organisations.

6.1 THE INCOME STATEMENT

We have looked at the balance sheet, which reports the company's investment in assets and how that investment is financed. We now consider the consequences of these management decisions as they are reflected in the income statement.

The income statement summarises the results of a company's productive activities in the course of an accounting period on an accrual basis, or its **earnings**. It reports the revenues invoiced (but not necessarily collected) from sales that were agreed during the period. The direct costs of the goods sold and the general expenses incurred (but not necessarily paid) are then deducted. The income statement records how the profit and loss reserve, or the earnings retained by the company, changed during the period.

The accruals basis is an example of the matching principle.

Public sector and not-for-profit organisations also have reason to produce income statements. Although they may not have the objective of making a profit (surplus), they may be required to:

(i) stay within their means i.e. income vs. expenditure

(ii) achieve a certain return on capital employed

(iii) build surpluses (reserves) for the future.

The income statement format presented in the OUFS also enumerates any other adjustments to shareholders' equity which are taken directly to reserves during the period, such as asset revaluations.

The consequences of operating and financing decisions of a similar type are grouped together within the income statement, as illustrated in Figure 6.1 overleaf. It is a simple exercise, therefore, to calculate sub-totals that allow us to evaluate these decisions.

Sales

– Cost of goods sold
– Selling and distribution expenses
– Administration expenses

Net operating profit

– Interest expense
+ Interest income
+ Equity income
+ Dividend income

Profit after financial items

+/– Sundry income/expense
+/– Gain/loss on sale of asset
+/– Gain/loss on sale of investment
+/– Exceptional income/expense

Pre-tax profit

– Tax

Net profit after tax

+/– Extraordinary income/expense
– Minority interests
– Dividends

Retained profit/loss for the year

Figure 6.1   The income statement. Shaded areas reflect financing decisions.

It is important to consider the implications of accruing revenues and expenses. As was indicated above, accruals mean that revenues and expenses may be reflected in the income statement before the cash is collected or disbursed. This creates the possibility of choice as to when revenues and expenses are included in the income statement.

'Not the "Yet-another-record-breaking-year" set, you fool! I want the "Just-about-keeping-our-heads-above-water" figures.'

Within the Anglo-American model, there are clear guidelines as to when revenues and expenses should be recognised in order to give a 'fair' view. Within the Franco-German model, companies are encouraged to take a very 'prudent' view and include revenues only when they are realised, but expenses as soon as they are anticipated. The Franco-German approach looks prudent or conservative in the year in which expenses are recognised, but they look anything but prudent in subsequent years when revenues are reflected without the associated expense. In the long term both practices will result in the same level of profit, but in a given year they can be very different.

Within the Franco-German model, profits can be reduced through the early recognition of expenses. Expenses may be included in the income statement before they have been incurred, and credited to an off-balance sheet provision. Expenses can be charged against this provision when they do occur. This practice has the effect of smoothing profits, reducing profit in buoyant times and enhancing profits in more difficult times.

The analyst has no simple means of identifying or translating the contrasting treatment of revenues and expenses, so comparisons of companies reporting under different models must be made with caution.

> The experience of Daimler-Benz, as already discussed in Unit 1, is a good example of the extent to which the timing of the recognition of revenues and expenses can differ. In the financial year 1993, Daimler-Benz showed a profit of DM615m under German rules, but losses of DM1.84bn under US rules. You can read more about this case in the Hawkins article in the Course Reader.

BOX 6.1 TURNOVER V. TOTAL COST

The income statement is always calculated on the basis of sales during the period within the Anglo-American model and is *often* calculated on the same basis within the Franco-German model. Within the Franco-German model, a company's income statement may focus on total production or total cost, rather than sales or turnover.

That is, the statement starts from sales and then adds the increase or decrease in inventories and own work capitalised. The expenses relate not to the goods sold but to total production. This is perfectly logical but it means that income statement ratios are not directly comparable between companies reporting on a total cost (par nature) format and those reporting on a turnover (par destination) format.

If you wish to make comparisons between companies which use different formats you can recalculate the turnover ratios which refer to cost of goods sold (i.e. inventory days), substituting the sales figure to give a ratio which can be compared.

6.2 PROFITABILITY RATIOS

Our starting point in assessing profitability is to consider the rate of growth or decline in sales. As the sales figure will reflect recent market prices, it is useful to compare the rate of growth in sales with the rate of inflation in order to see if there has been growth in the volume of production. When interpreting this volume, you should bear in mind that the sales figure will include revenues from businesses acquired (or sold) from (or up to) the date of the acquisition (disposal). If your objective is to estimate possible future rates of growth, you must adjust for sales gained (or lost) through acquisition (or disposals) to identify the underlying trends in the existing business.

Interpreting the trend in sales can pose a particular problem for companies trading in many countries. Typically, sales figures are translated (or converted to the reported currency) at the exchange rates achieved during the period. The figure will therefore include not only price and volume changes but also exchange rate changes.

Companies occasionally provide a comparison giving sales and operating profit at constant exchange rates to help readers interpret the numbers.

BOX 6.2 CARNAUDMETALBOX – EXTRACT FROM THE 1993 ANNUAL REPORT AND ACCOUNTS

EXCHANGE RATE IMPACT ON 1993 RESULTS

The Sterling, Lira and Peseta 1992 devaluations combined with the depreciation of certain African currencies relative to the French Franc during the year have significantly influenced the 1993 results.

Had the 1992 average exchange rates been applied in 1993, Carnaud's results would have been as follows:

	1993 Actual (FRFm)	1993 at 1992 exch. rates (FRFm)	1992 Actual (FRFm)
Turnover	23,340	25,504	24,830
Operating profit	2,058	2,195	2,454
Profit on ordinary activities	1,495	1,602	1,812
Profit after taxation	1,022	1,096	1,250
Attributable profits	835	895	976

Net operating profit

Many of the ratios that focus on profitability relate sub-totals from the income statement to the overall level of sales. The first profitability ratio looks at the net operating profit:

$$\frac{\text{Net operating profit}}{\text{Sales}} \times 100$$

This is a key ratio showing us a company's basic operating performance or core income. It is the net revenues arising from the company's cycle of production. It represents only the company's core or sustainable revenues before the financing decisions or one-off events, good or bad. It is therefore our usual starting point in assessing what we expect to happen in the future.

In order to gain a deeper understanding of the components of net operating profit, we may look at the two major categories of expenses deducted from sales to give net operating profit:

$$\frac{\text{Cost of goods sold}}{\text{Sales}} \times 100$$

$$\frac{\text{Selling and distribution expenses}}{\text{Sales}} \times 100$$

The first ratio looks at the direct costs of output and can help to highlight any changes in the efficiency of the production process or market-influenced changes in gross margin. The second ratio focuses on the general expenses associated with selling. It is an important ratio to monitor since bad debts are often considered to be part of the cost of selling and any deterioration in collection experience may be reflected in this ratio.

Interest cover

Operating profit levels are then compared to the figure that is typically the largest obligatory external financial charge, interest expense. The ratio which is normally calculated is 'times interest earned' or interest cover:

$$\frac{\text{Net operating profit}}{\text{Interest expense}}$$

While this ratio is widely quoted it has two serious shortcomings:

(i)   The ratio looks at profit, which is an accrued figure, relative to interest expense, which is a cash obligation.

(ii) Debt providers require not only payment of interest but also repayment of principal on schedule.

We will consider alternative ratios that address these shortcomings when we look at cash flow ratios in Section 8.3.

Pre-tax profit

The next sub-total that we consider is pre-tax profit, which we relate to the level of sales:

$$\frac{\text{Pre-tax profit}}{\text{Sales}} \times 100$$

We then focus on the percentage of those earnings paid in taxes:

$$\text{Effective tax rate} = \frac{\text{Taxes}}{\text{Pre-tax profit}} \times 100$$

This rate can vary considerably, since companies operate in different markets that are subject to different tax regimes. The analyst should always be wary of low tax rates and investigate them closely. Within the Anglo-American model, tax accounts and published accounts are different. The tax authorities generally have access to more information than is included in the published accounts. When tax rates are low it may be that the tax authorities consider the earnings to be lower than those which are reported in the published accounts. The user must look carefully to ensure that earnings are not being 'enhanced' in some way.

In order to encourage investment, tax regulations often allow companies to write off the cost of capital goods at a faster rate than they are actually being consumed, thereby delaying the

'Instead of my usual report, I've written a little song about our accounting procedure, our lack of cash flow, and why the business is going to hell in a handbasket. Feel free to jump in on the chorus.'

payment of tax. In the Franco-German bloc this means that a company often owns plant and equipment which is in good working order and has a real market value, but does not appear on the balance sheet as it has been fully written off. The economic value of this fully written-off capital equipment represents a hidden reserve for the company.

Accelerated capital consumption allowances are also common in countries using the Anglo-American model. **Capital allowances** for tax purposes may therefore differ from depreciation on a 'fair' basis shown in the accounts. The difference in the tax that is actually payable and the tax that would have been payable if capital allowances had been equal to the depreciation shown in the accounts is shown as deferred taxation.

BOX 6.3   UK ADVANCE CORPORATION TAX

Within the UK, a company paying dividends has, until recently, been required to pay the tax authorities an amount equal to the basic tax rate on those dividends. (You will see these payments in the financial statements of the companies used as examples in this course.) This payment could be offset against future corporate tax liabilities, but could not be reclaimed. If a company paid dividends in the UK but earned income overseas, this caused a considerable problem. The payment (Advance Corporation Tax) was incurred when dividends were paid, but there might be no liability for UK corporation tax against which the tax prepayment might be set in the foreseeable future. The scale of this tax prepayment was significant and led to substantial periodic write-offs when there was no reasonable chance of recovering sums. Advance Corporation Tax was abolished in the UK in 1998.

Net profit after tax

The profits attributable to shareholders are net profit after tax. This sub-total can be related to the level of sales:

$$\frac{\text{Net profit after tax}}{\text{Sales}} \times 100$$

We then turn to look at the percentage of these after-tax profits that were paid to shareholders in the form of dividends:

$$\text{Payout ratio} = \frac{\text{Dividends}}{\text{Net profit after tax}} \times 100$$

Unit 4 contains more on dividend policy, which is at the management's discretion.

The payout ratio depends on the going rate in the industry and the value of dividends in previous years. In practice, companies are reluctant to cut dividends to a value below that paid in previous years or even to break an established growth pattern, whether or not the payment is justified by the current performance. The payout ratio serves as an alarm to warn when dividends do not reflect the trend in underlying earnings.

6.3   CORE V. NON-CORE EARNINGS

It is useful at this stage to introduce the concept of 'core earnings', or earnings arising directly from the company's management of its cycle of production. Focusing on the income statement, we can see that the revenues and expenses related directly to the cycle of production have been included at the net operating profit level.

Non-core income/expense includes all income and expenses below net operating profit level. Non-core income includes income and expense arising from financial decisions, as well as one-off expenses and revenues arising from operating decisions. The distinction between core and non-core income is crucial when we turn to forecasting and our principal aim is to identify those revenues and expenses that we expect to see repeated in future periods.

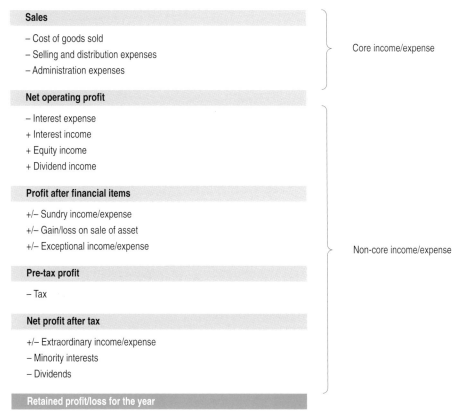

Figure 6.2   Core and non-core earnings

6.4 MARKET-RELATED RATIOS

There are several ratios that relate the earnings of a company to the number and market price of its shares.

Earnings per share

Earnings per share calculates the earnings at the level of net profit after tax attributable to each share:

$$\text{Earnings per share} = \frac{\text{Net profit after tax}}{\text{Average number of shares issued}}$$

Earnings per share is often related to the price of acquiring that share through the calculation of the price earnings ratio:

$$\text{Price/earnings ratio} = \frac{\text{Market price of share}}{\text{Earnings per share}}$$

Analysts often make adjustments to these simple definitions of earnings per share and price/earnings ratio. Since any potential investor is buying a right to future earnings, analysts often look at these ratios as they relate to expected future earnings by estimating a prospective price/earnings ratio:

$$\text{Prospective price/earnings ratio} = \frac{\text{Market price of share}}{\text{Expected earnings per share}}$$

Analysts may also adjust the reported historic earnings to eliminate any earnings related to abnormal items, events or accounting policies. The definition of such 'normalised' earnings may vary from analyst to analyst, but it generally includes adjustments similar to those recommended by the UK-based Institute of Investment Management and Research:

- remove capital items and items of an abnormal nature
- provide fully for deferred taxation
- deduct capitalised items that would normally be charged to the income statement.

Price/book ratio

The price of a share reflects a consensus view of the present value of the future earnings of a company. The book value of shareholders' equity reflects the historic cost or the current market value of assets. These two estimates of the value of a company can be expected to differ. The relationship between these alternative valuations is compared directly by the ratio Price/Book, which relates the market price of a share to the book value of shareholders' equity per share:

$$\text{Price/book} = \frac{\text{Market share price}}{\text{Shareholders' equity per share}}$$

The price/book ratio can also be calculated at the company rather than the share level, using market capitalisation:

$$\text{Price/book} = \frac{\text{Market capitalisation}}{\text{Shareholders' equity}}$$

Market capitalisation (which is share price multiplied by the number of shares in issue) is often used as the measure of the size of a company instead of accounting measures such as total assets or operating profit, which can be distorted by different accounting practices.

6.5   OTHER OUTPUT-RELATED PERFORMANCE INDICATORS

The profitability measures that summarise the performance of firms in the private sector are not directly applicable to the public sector and other not-for-profit (NFP) organisations. However, a similar ratio analysis approach can be used to assess the performance of charities (for example, Save the Children or the Federation of Festivals for Music, Speech and Drama), lobbying organisations (for example, Friends of the Earth) or service providers in the public sector (for example, UK National Health Service Trusts), that have identifiable objectives other than maximising shareholder return. All these organisations receive revenues and incur expenses in order to achieve some outcome and produce financial statements reflecting these activities. As they have objectives, it is of interest to their managers, contributors and monitoring agencies to know how efficiently the companies are pursuing their objectives.

The possibility of using ratio analysis in these instances depends on identifying a measurable outcome that is the agreed objective of the organisation and devising a system of accountability relating to the agreed objective. This is an easier task for some NFP organisations than others. For example, it is easier to measure the number of people attending or participating in festivals associated with the Federation of Festivals for Music, Speech and Drama than it is to measure the environmental pollution prevented by Friends of the Earth. Output-related performance indicators (ORPIs) potentially play an important role in improving and monitoring performance, but the choice and detailed definition of an appropriate ORPI can pose a complex challenge.

Unless the ORPI is very carefully designed, it may reveal little about progress toward the 'true' objective and may also divert effort and resources. Consider, for example, an aid agency that wishes to provide fresh drinking water in the poorest regions in the world. One quantifiable target might be to maximise the number of wells drilled. Another might be to maximise the number of people given improved access to fresh water. Still another might be to maximise the number of hours saved in walking to collect daily water supplies. The target might also be an indirect one such as the reduction of infant mortality rates. The administrative cost of achieving each of these targets is not the same, nor is the benefit in terms of human welfare. You could drill a maximum number of wells for a given outlay by selecting the easiest geological conditions. You could maximise the number of people benefiting by siting the wells in a population centre. Maximising the number of hours saved in walking to collect daily water supplies would require a large investment in research to site the wells, but could bring the greatest welfare gains. Reduction in infant mortality rates may also bring huge welfare gains but it is unlikely that any changes could be solely attributed to the improved availability of fresh water.

BOX 6.4 OUTPUT-RELATED PERFORMANCE INDICATORS

There is a large body of literature related to the use of output performance data in the public sector. A good example is provided by Peter Smith (1993) in an article in which he summarises the use of ORPIs in the UK's National Health Service and identifies seven ways in which inappropriate definitions and application of output-related performance indicators were observed to misdirect effort:

(i)   *Tunnel vision* – Concentration on areas included in the ORPI scheme to the exclusion of other important areas.

(ii) *Sub-optimisation* – The pursuit by managers of their own narrow objectives at the expense of strategic co-ordination.

(iii) *Myopia* – Concentration on short-term issues to the exclusion of long-term criteria, which may only show up in the ORPI in many years' time.

(iv) *Convergence* – An emphasis on not being exposed as an outlier on any ORPI, rather than a desire to be outstanding.

(v)   *Ossification* – A disinclination to experiment with new and innovative methods.

(vi) *Gaming* – Altering behaviour so as to obtain strategic advantage.

(vii) *Misrepresentation* – Including 'creative' accounting and fraud.

Activity 6.1

Read the article by Andrew Likierman in the Course Reader. The article provides a practical guide to defining and using ORPIs in the public and NFP sectors.

As the consideration of possible 'measures' for the objective of providing fresh drinking water illustrates, great care should be taken in identifying the quantifiable target. If an inappropriate target is selected, there is a risk that efforts and resources will be directed away from the objective. Using our example, drilling the maximum number of wells may not be consistent with bringing fresh water to the maximum number of people or producing the greatest gains in human welfare.

Provided that an appropriate quantifiable outcome can be identified, we can calculate the investment needed to achieve each unit of the agreed target. We can compare this to the organisation's own performance over time or with similar organisations (if they exist).

Most NFPs also quote the proportion of money raised that goes to beneficiaries and the proportion that goes to administration. It should be kept in mind that a maximum percentage payout to beneficiaries may not be consistent with a maximum outcome if it means that funds are inappropriately allocated or programmes are inexpertly implemented.

NFPs often must invest in order to raise funds, whether through advertising or organising fund-raising events. The efficiency of this aspect of their operations is monitored by calculating the ratio of funds raised to the investment in fund-raising activities.

A ratio that is of interest for any organisation implementing long-term projects is the percentage of allocated funds held in reserve. Delays in implementing or completing a project can impose huge costs. For example, delaying a capital project such as a dam may lead to the deterioration of work completed to that point and the dispersal of engineering and construction teams.

Stability of funding over time is an important consideration for many NFPs implementing medium- to long-term projects. It is therefore useful to focus on the proportion of funds raised by single events or contributions, relative to the proportion of funds raised through a continuing relationship with donors, such as membership, covenants or child sponsorship.

BOX 6.5   ACTIONAID

It is instructive to review the ratios published and monitored by ActionAid, a UK based charity existing to help children, families and communities in the world's poorest countries overcome poverty and secure lasting improvements in the quality of their lives. These aims are achieved through programmes providing access to vital services such as clean water, primary healthcare and education, and encouraging local economic development.

The report distributed to contributors includes the following ratios:

Income by source	%
Sponsorship	57
Official income	21
Donations and appeals	13
Affiliates	7
Trading/miscellaneous	2
Total	**100**

Expenditure by use	%
Development work	66
Influencing education/research	5
Emergencies	13
Administration	2
Fundraising	14
Total	**100**

ActionAid specify a policy of keeping reserves of at least one quarter of the following year's planned expenditure for each development project. These funds are held in the UK and invested to generate further income.

They also calculate a five-year rolling average of expenditure on fundraising and administration, most recently 15.7%, leaving 84% of income for development work.

The agency monitors, but does not publish, central administration and local administration costs as a proportion of total project costs. Projects and programmes are monitored where possible – for example, the effectiveness of literacy programmes is evaluated by assessing the reading skills retained after one year.

Exercise 6.1 _____

The Albert Fisher Group plc is a UK-based food group operating throughout the world in the sourcing, processing and distribution of fruit, vegetables and seafood. During the four years to 30 August 1996, the group undertook a programme of strategic repositioning, enhancing customer relationships, strengthening management and reducing their risk profile. During this period the management's stated policy was to 'focus on added value' by developing businesses producing processed output and moving away from simple food distribution.

In 1996, the group had a non-operating exceptional charge of £151.0m that related to the termination or disposal of businesses as part of the strategic repositioning. As this charge is exceptional (or a 'one-off'), it has been added back to net profit before tax and net profit after tax, to give a fairer picture of the underlying performance of the group's continuing operations. Using the adjusted information provided below, calculate adjusted profitability ratios for The Albert Fisher Group in 1996. Assess Albert Fisher's performance on the basis of these ratios and the information on previous years provided in Appendix 4.

Sales	1,697.9
Cost of goods sold	(1,463.8)
Selling and distribution expense	(118.7)
Net operating profit	47.6
Interest expense	(18.4)
Pre-tax profit (before exceptionals)	40.1
Tax	10.4
Net profit after tax (before exceptionals)	29.7
Dividends	(26.8)
Shareholders' equity	148.8

SUMMARY

In this section we reviewed the ratios that assess the performance of a company as reflected in its income statement. The ratios relate costs and margins to the level of sales or calculate how easily specific categories of cost are covered by profits. The distinction between core and non-core income was discussed, and the importance of distinguishing between recurring and non-recurring income was reviewed. The significance of different accounting practices regarding the timing of the recognition of expenses and thus profits was outlined. Finally, other performance measures that can be used to assess the performance of NFP organisations were considered.

7 RATIO ANALYSIS

Sections 4, 5 and 6 examined in some detail the ratios and related measures that can help you evaluate the financial performance of a company in the three key areas, operating efficiency, **financial structure** and profitability. We now look at **core ratios**, which summarise the performance in each of these areas in a *single* ratio; the overall performance of the company is summarised as the product of these core ratios. As well as helping to integrate your analysis of a company, the simple core ratio model serves to highlight the major areas of change or concern and thus provides a very useful signpost to the areas where further investigation is required.

At the end of this section you should be able to:

- define the core ratios
- outline the logic of the OUFS ratio sheet format.

7.1 THE CORE RATIOS

So far in Book 2, we have looked separately at the operating efficiency, financial structure and profitability of a company.

The Return on Capital Employed (ROCE) ratio combines two of these aspects of a company's performance, operating efficiency and profitability.

$$\text{ROCE} = \frac{\text{Net Operating Profit}}{\text{Capital Employed}} \times 100$$

Net operating profit is before interest and tax. Capital employed is the total long term debt and equity invested in the company.

From your previous studies you may be aware of the so-called Dupont Pyramid which breaks ROCE down into the component parts of efficiency and profitability by calculating one form of Return on Sales and the Asset Utilisation ratio.

Dupont Pyramid

Return on equity	=	Operating efficiency	×	Profitability

or

Return on Capital Employed	=	Asset utilisation	×	Return on sales

or

$$\frac{\text{Net operating profit}}{\text{Capital employed}} = \frac{\text{Sales}}{\text{Capital employed}} \times \frac{\text{Net operating profit}}{\text{Sales}}$$

However, this analysis fails to consider the financial structure of the company, which is the other major aspect of a company's financial performance. It also looks at the performance of the company from the perspective of both long term debt and equity investors.

If we wish to consider the company's performance from the shareholders' perspective then we need to consider not the ROCE, but the return on equity, which we can define numerically as net profit after tax/equity. This return on equity reflects how well the company has been managed in the three areas open to management – operating efficiency, financial structure and profitability. The performance in each of these three areas can also be expressed in a single simple ratio, operating efficiency as sales/total assets (asset turnover), financial structure as total assets/equity (asset leverage) and profitability as net profit after tax/sales (an alternative version of return on sales). Expressed in this form we see that the mathematical product of the three key ratios is return on equity (measured as net profit after tax/equity).

These ratios provide an invaluable summary of the major trends in the key areas in which management's performance may be assessed,

Core Ratios

Return on equity	=	Operating efficiency	×	Financial structure	×	Profitability

or

Return on equity	=	Asset turnover	×	Asset leverage	×	Return on sales

or

$$\frac{NPAT}{Equity} = \frac{Sales}{Total\ assets} \times \frac{Total\ assets}{Equity} \times \frac{NPAT}{Sales}$$

indicating at a glance where users of financial statements should direct their attention. Since users of financial statements are often overwhelmed by the wealth of information provided, these core ratios provide a helpful guide to highlight the aspects of a company's performance where the users will find the major problems, changes or trends. Having identified the key areas of change or concern, you can then turn to the block of more detailed ratios for those areas to gain insight into the significance of the problems, changes or trends you have identified.

Exercise 7.1 _____

Why is the return on sales in the Dupont Pyramid defined as:

$$\frac{Net\ operating\ profit}{Sales} \times 100\%$$

whereas the return on sales in the core ratios is defined as

$$\frac{Net\ profit\ after\ tax}{Sales} \times 100\%$$

7.2 INTERPRETING THE CORE RATIOS

BOX 7.1   INTERPRETING FINANCIAL RATIOS

(i)   Do the ratios make sense?

(ii)   How do the ratios compare with those reported by similar companies?

(iii) How have the ratios changed over time?

Following the sequence of the three questions set out in Box 7.1, you can readily identify how the underlying core ratios have changed over time and how they compare with the performance of similar companies over time. In order to reach a conclusion as to whether the pattern of ratios makes sense, you must first have some idea of the pattern you expect to see. While experience undoubtedly provides greater understanding of the patterns characteristic of an industry and its economic circumstances, common sense can give even novice users a reasonable guide.

In any sector the returns shareholders demand, measured as the return on equity, will exceed the returns available on a relatively risk-free investment (e.g. government bond, bank deposit) by an amount reflecting the 'risk', in terms of the expected variability of profits, in that sector. The greater the risk, the greater the required return.

In contrast, the underlying core ratios determining return on equity should be expected to vary widely between sectors and also among companies within a sector depending on the strategy each has adopted.

The level of asset turnover (defined as sales/total assets) must reflect the technology of the sector; technology will determine the assets that are required to conduct a given business. An advertising agency needs only a modest asset investment to conduct its business, while a car manufacturer needs substantial investment in plant and machinery to produce a vehicle. However, there will be also be room for variation within a sector reflecting management choices given the technology. For example, a company may choose between a specialised niche and a low cost/high volume strategy with the two strategies requiring different asset investments.

The asset leverage (defined as total assets/equity) should be inversely related to the volatility of cash flows generated. The greater the uncertainty of revenues, the greater the proportion of the company's asset investment that should be funded through equity and so the lower the asset leverage. Thus, an advertising agency (which depends on the creative inspiration of employees who could leave the agency or fail to find inspiration) might be expected to have a low level of asset leverage. A car manufacturer, with an established market position that can also offer lenders a security interest in a large pool of fixed assets, might be expected to have a relatively high level of asset leverage.

The profitability (defined as net profit after tax/sales) reflects a range of sector characteristics that were outlined in some detail in the discussion of the Porter model in Section 3. While there are exceptions, profitability generally follows the rule of thumb that the longer the cycle of production and the greater the value added, the higher the profitability. Thus, a high street fashion retailer (purchasing finished goods and selling them on very quickly) would be expected to report relatively modest profitability, while a property developer would be expected to have higher profitability to compensate for the uncertainty inherent in a long cycle of production.

A quick review of these summary figures can confirm whether or not a company is following the expected pattern; if it is not, then the reasons for the variation from the expected pattern can be explored.

7.3 INTERPRETING THE CORE RATIOS – AN ILLUSTRATION

To illustrate how the core ratios can help the users of financial statements, let us consider the core ratios calculated for The Albert Fisher Group plc for the five years to August 1996, which have been adjusted, as in Exercise 6.1, to reflect profits before exceptional items.

Table 7.1 The Albert Fisher Group plc – core ratios					
	30.8.92	30.8.93	30.8.94	30.8.95	30.8.96
Return on sales	0.85%	1.44%	1.54%	1.26%	1.75%
Asset turnover	1.92	2.47	2.35	2.67	2.73
Asset leverage	2.35	2.89	3.11	3.55	4.18
Return on equity	3.83%	10.32%	11.26%	11.92%	19.96%

At that time Albert Fisher was involved in food processing and distribution in Europe and North America. During this five-year period, the management's stated policy was to reposition the group, 'focusing on added value', by developing the businesses producing processed output and moving away from simple food distribution businesses.

Food processing and distribution is a competitive business, with many small players. Any specific food has many close substitutes, and the food processors' main customers in Europe and North America are the large, concentrated supermarket chains. Food processors have no power over the many fragmented suppliers of agricultural products and they must cope with dramatic variations in the supply of raw materials as a result of the impact of unpredictable weather on crops. There is limited brand identification for a food manufacturer, with supermarket 'own brands' competing with any manufacturer's brand names. All these factors would lead us to expect a relatively low level of profitability in this sector.

Turning to the core ratios, we might expect Albert Fisher's move to higher value-added processed products would increase a relatively low return on sales. The ratio did rise, doubling from a very low level of 0.85% to 1.75% at the end of the period. At 1.75%, the return on sales remained modest, but that is consistent with our expectations for this sector.

We might expect to find, and accept, a decreasing level of asset turnover during this period as Albert Fisher moved to higher value-added products with a longer cycle of production. In fact, Albert Fisher reported an increase in asset turnover, from 1.92 to 2.73, during the period.

The price and availability of agricultural commodities, Albert Fisher's raw materials, inevitably vary. These cost variations cannot be passed on to the powerful supermarket chains or the final consumer who can easily switch to similar food products. We might therefore expect to see a relatively low level of asset leverage, with an 'equity cushion' to ensure Albert Fisher's survival when raw materials are expensive and in short supply. During this period, asset leverage rose from an already high level of 2.35 to 4.18.

The overall consequences of Albert Fisher's management strategy during the period are seen in the dramatic increase in return on equity from 3.83% at the start of the period to 19.96% at the end of the period. This impressive increase, however, has not been achieved solely through the stated objective of developing higher value-added products, but through increasing the financial risk in an inevitably cyclical and variable industry. Assets are also being used more efficiently.

The core ratios highlight two major issues that must be investigated by examining the blocks of related ratios in greater detail and comparing Albert Fisher's performance to that of its peers during the same period:

(i) Can profit margins continue to be sustained and increased by the current strategy?

(ii) Is the financial risk too great given the characteristics of the industry?

This brief examination of the core ratios has provided a focus for our more detailed examination of Albert Fisher's performance and the specific areas where we may gain insight by comparing Albert Fisher's performance to that of its peers.

Exercise 7.2

The following problem will allow you to exercise your common sense and provide practice in using core ratios to evaluate performance.

Eight sectors are listed in Table 7.2. The table that follows gives 'company profiles' of eight UK companies. The company profiles provide a percentage breakdown of the assets and liabilities included in the financial statements, as well as the core ratios for each company. Examine the company profiles and suggest the sector to which each profile belongs.

Industry	Company
Airline	❏
Supermarket chain	❏
Advertising agency group	❏
Holding company	❏
High street retailer	❏
Bank	❏
Hotel and casino chain	❏
Electrical utility	❏

Table 7.2 Company profiles	A	B	C	D	E	F	G	H
Core ratios								
Return on equity	15.87%	N/A	6.4%	13.5%	(110.0%)	7.9%	17.2%	18.96%
Return on sales	9.04%	N/A	13.6%	4.0%	10.0%	2.6%	N/A	6.09%
Asset turnover	1.1388	N/A	0.3232	1.78	3.5	1.1320	N/A	0.7728
Asset leverage	1.5414	N/A	1.4477	1.91	(30.1)	2.6960	23.333	4.0261
Balance Sheet %								
Cash and marketable securities	17.0	–	1.2	3.2	20.0	11.1	8.5	12.0
Trade receivables	7.5	0.3	1.6	0.8	38.5	9.8	78.9	9.9
Inventory	6.7	–	0.3	11.3	4.9	0.7	–	1.0
Other current assets	3.3	–	0.9	2.0	7.5	2.3	–	3.8
Property, plant and equipment	54.0	–	94.4	80.8	7.4	72.6	1.8	68.0
Investments	0.7	97.1	0.6	1.7	1.9	1.7	1.9	5.3
Intangibles	–	–	–	–	18.6	–	–	–
Other assets	10.8	2.6	1.0	0.2	1.2	1.8	8.9	–
Total assets	100.0	100.0	100.0	100.0	100.0	100.0	100.0	100.0
Short-term debt	7.8	–	3.1	12.0	3.8	9.4	80.7	3.6
Trade creditors	3.1	13.0	3.2	12.1	53.6	9.8	–	10.2
Accrued expenses	3.3	–	1.6	2.2	14.5	4.8	1.4	1.3
Other current liabilities	12.2	1.4	2.4	11.0	8.9	8.9	8.5	13.0
Long-term debt	7.8	–	20.7	9.4	12.4	23.7	2.8	45.3
Other long-term liabilities	0.9	–	–	1.0	10.1	6.3	2.3	1.7
Ordinary shares and share premium	14.6	70.1	29.7	22.7	25.7	11.7	1.9	7.1
Reserves	50.3	15.5	39.3	29.6	(29.0)	25.4	2.4	17.8
Total liabilities and equity	100.0	100.0	100.0	100.0	100.0	100.0	100.0	100.0

SUMMARY

The core ratios demonstrate the mathematical relationships between the measures of a company's operating efficiency, financial structure and profitability. By summarising the performance of a company in these areas, and its overall performance in return on equity, the core ratios provide a picture of its performance at a glance. The patterns reflected in the core ratios provide an invaluable tool for analysts by highlighting the areas of a company's performance where further investigation is needed.

8 CASH FLOW

As we have seen, ratios based on the income statement or the balance sheet fail to provide an answer to the key question 'Can all payments be made as they fall due?'. The importance of this question is clear when you consider that if a company is not able to meet its financial obligations, it risks going out of business. A company can, of course, raise cash in the short term by selling assets or borrowing funds, but in the medium to long term the cash from operations must be sufficient to cover the financial obligations arising from these operations or it cannot survive.

The accounting statement which focuses on the sources and uses of cash during an accounting period is called the cash flow statement. Increasingly, accounting regulations require companies to publish cash flow statements but the requirement is far from universal; they are not required in many European jurisdictions and in the UK they are only required for larger companies.

If a company does not publish a cash flow statement it is a relatively simple exercise to estimate, or derive, a cash flow on the basis of information published elsewhere in the financial statements. Understanding this derivation will ensure that analysts will always be able to focus on this crucial aspect of a company's performance.

The calculation has three objectives:

(i)   to identify the sources and uses of cash (as distinct from accrued revenues and expenses)

(ii)   to separate the sources and uses of cash arising from the company's core operations (and therefore likely to be repeated) from those arising from peripheral activities or unusual events (and therefore not likely to be repeated)

(iii)   to calculate sub-totals that help us compare the cash generated by the company with the cash required by it.

There are as many formats used to organise a derived cash flow as there are analysts. We will use a format which provides a financial 'health check' and provides sub-totals which will be used later in the course for forecasting corporate performance and calculating corporate valuations. Other formats are equally valid and a company-prepared cash flow statement may be better in that it may reflect information which is not available for the calculation of a derived cash flow. None the less we will focus on a derived cash flow because it provides a sort of 'common denominator' that is always available to the analyst.

We begin this section by outlining the calculation of a derived cash flow, illustrating this with the calculation of a cash flow for Albert Fisher plc. We consider the adjustments that are required if an historical cash flow is to be used as the basis for forecasting future cash flows. We then turn to the cash flow ratios that assess the financial health of a company. The final section uses Albert Fisher to illustrate the interpretation of a cash flow and its associated ratios.

At the end of this section you should be able to:

- summarise the advantages of cash flow statements over income statements
- outline the logic of the OUFS spreadsheet cash flow statement
- calculate a simple derived cash flow statement
- understand the logic of cash flow ratios.

8.1   CALCULATING THE OUFS DERIVED CASH FLOW

This section explains the calculation of a derived cash flow and illustrates the process by calculating the 1996 cash flow for Albert Fisher on the basis of the 1996 financial statements. You will find an OUFS printout showing the financial statements for the company in Appendix 4. The line references listed in these calculations refer you to the line in the OUFS where you will find the figures used in the calculation.

Operating profit

Our calculation of a derived cash flow starts with operating profit. Operating profit represents the accrued revenues associated with sales for the year less accrued direct costs and overhead expenses. The first step is to make adjustments for (or add back) any non-cash items that have been deducted in calculating operating profit. Depreciation is the most frequently encountered example of such non-cash deductions, but other similar deductions should be treated in the same way – for example, amortisation, depletion or provisions.

This allows us to calculate a sub-total that is called 'earnings before interest, taxes, depreciation and amortisation' (**EBITDA**). While EBITDA is still a combination of some accrued and some cash revenues and expenses, it is a figure that is often used in valuations, particularly when comparing companies in a particular sector across national borders. Its attraction is that it strips out the distorting effect of differing depreciation policies, capital structures and tax regimes.

	OUFS line ref.	£m
Net operating profit	336	47.6
+ Depreciation	320	19.4
= EBITDA		67.0

Our next step is to make adjustments for any accrued revenues and expenses relating to current operations. We can estimate the cash sources and the uses relating to operating assets in the following way. Consider first trade receivables. We know how much the company was owed by its customers at the start of the period by looking at the closing balance of the previous period. We also know how much the company is owed by customers at the end of this period. If the level has gone up, we know that some of the trade receivables relating to the current year cannot have been collected. An increase between the opening and closing balance of trade receivables tells us the value of trade receivables that have not been collected and we can reduce accrued revenues by this amount (a use of cash). If the level of trade receivables has come down in the course of the year, we know that the company must have collected all of this year's trade receivables as well as some of those relating to the previous year. A decline in the level of trade receivables provides a source of cash over and above the year's sales, and an equal amount can be added to the accrued revenues (a source of cash).

	OUFS line ref.	£m
Trade receivables at the start of the period	117	143.9
Trade receivables at the end of the period	117	(139.3)
Additional source (use) of cash		4.6

A similar logic can be applied to changes between the opening and closing balances of operating liabilities, except that an increase in an operating liability such as trade creditors represents a source of cash (or additional credit) while a decline represents a use of cash (or a repayment of past credit). So an increase in an asset or a decrease in a liability is a cash outflow (or use of cash), while a decrease in an asset or an increase in a liability is a cash inflow (or a source of cash).

All the changes in the opening and closing balances of all categories of operating assets and liabilities can be added together to show the additional sources and uses of cash arising from current operations. The sources and uses of cash arising from the movement in net operating assets are of interest because they show us the cash consequences of management's decisions concerning those factors that they are able to influence in the short term.

	OUFS line ref.	£m
Change in trade receivables	117	4.6
Change in inventory	125	(13.4)
Change in trade creditors	218	(15.7)
Change in accrued expenses	219	1.6
Change in prepaid expenses	136	1.9
Additional source (use) from net operating assets		(21.0)

Changes in other current assets and liabilities may be added to the additional sources and uses from net operating assets to calculate the additional sources and uses from changes in working capital.

By adjusting EBITDA for the additional sources or uses of cash arising from movements in working capital, we will have a sub-total called

Operating Cash Flow. This sub-total is the starting point, or top line, of the cash flow statement in UK accounts.

	OUFS line ref.	£m
EBITDA	514	67.0
+/– Additional sources (uses) from net operating assets	520	(21.0)
+/– Additional sources (uses) from other current assets	521	2.5
+/– Additional sources (uses) from other current liabilities	522	11.8
Operating Cash Flow (OCF)	523	60.3

Operating cash flow is interesting because it shows the cash that is being generated by a company's operations before financing decisions and long-term investment decisions. It represents the cash that is coming from operations before making any investment for the future, or making any payment to lenders and investors. Many of the cash flow ratios that we calculate show how well this available cash covers obligatory cash payments and investments for future production.

The next set of cash flows that we examine are the contractual or non-discretionary payments that the company *must* make during the period.

Tax is the first non-discretionary payment that we consider. The tax payment included in the income statement relates to that fiscal year, but the cash payment is usually made quite a long time after the financial year-end – about 18 months later in the UK. It is therefore necessary to do some additional calculations to estimate how much *cash* was actually paid in taxes during the period. We start by looking at the tax that was owed (or payable) at the start of the period, add the additional tax liability incurred during the period and subtract the tax that remains unpaid at the end of the period. This calculation must also take into account any tax payments that may have been made relating to earnings in past years (such as deferred taxation) or future years (such as the UK's Advance Corporation Tax).

	OUFS line ref.	£m	£m
Corporation tax payable at the start of the period	222, 246	(15.8)	
Corporation tax liability for the period	353, 354	(9.5)	
Corporation tax payable at the end of the period	222, 246	19.1	
Sub-total: cash corporation tax paid during the period			(6.2)
Deferred tax payable at the start of the period	251	(1.1)	
Deferred tax liability for the period	355	(0.5)	
Deferred tax payable at the end of the period	251	1.5	
Sub-total: deferred tax paid during the period			(0.1)
Tax prepayments at the start of the period	165		3.4
Tax prepayments at the end of the period	165		(3.4)
Other tax/prior year adjustment	356, 357		(0.4)
Total: Taxes paid	524		(6.7)

The next set of cash flows that we consider are the contractual payments associated with the company's debt. For these purposes we consider the payments associated with both debt and finance leases. Lenders usually require interest to be paid regularly (often quarterly or semi-annually) so that they can meet the needs of their own funding providers. Interest is therefore not usually accrued, but expended during the year. There are occasional exceptions where accrued interest is found on the balance sheet (such as bonds issued at a deep discount) but interest and lease expense can normally be taken from the income statement.

Repayments required under the terms of loan or lease agreements are the second category of cash flows associated with debt and leases. Most accounting standards require companies to identify how much of their debt is due for repayment in the following year (often called the 'current portion'), so, by looking at the previous year's balance sheet, we can see how much cash must be repaid during the period we are considering. It is sometimes argued that these payments can be ignored, since a bank will want to renew a loan if the company is doing well, and will be forced to accept a new repayment schedule if the company cannot repay on time. It is a brave analyst who assumes that the lenders will always take such a fatalistic view. The scale of loan repayments can be very large relative to the cash generated in a single period. The recession of the early 1990s provided many examples of banks putting companies into liquidation or imposing severe restrictions on management in restructuring debt rather than simply accepting extended repayment terms. We therefore include mandatory repayments of debt and leases as non-discretionary payments.

	OUFS line ref.	£m
Operating cash flow	523	60.3
Taxes paid	524	(6.7)
Interest paid	337	(18.4)
Current portion of long-term debt and leases (previous year)	215, 216	(28.6)
Discretionary cash flow	527	6.6

Discretionary cash flow represents the cash available to the firm after current operations and after meeting obligatory payments.

We now consider how the firm may choose to use the available cash.

The first discretionary payment we consider is the dividend payment. Although a company is not contractually obliged to pay dividends, you should consider whether it is obliged to make dividend payments in practice. As we will see in greater detail in Unit 4, dividends are often used as a means of signalling future prospects and managers are loath to cut or cancel dividends since the market tends to react dramatically to negative news. In reality, cash flow *after* dividends (cash flow before long-term uses) *may* represent the cash which is truly at management's discretion.

	OUFS line ref.	£m
Discretionary cash flow	527	6.6
Dividends payable at the start of the period	225	(13.6)
Dividends declared during the period	363	(26.8)
Dividends still payable at the end of the period	225	13.6
Cash flow before long-term uses	529	(20.2)

We now turn to consider how the company *chose* to spend its remaining cash. The largest expense is often associated with the purchase of property, plant and equipment (at this point we have not even made provision for the minimum capital expenditure that would be required to maintain the business). Again, although it is not a contractual obligation, most companies would wither on the vine if they failed to replace and maintain their productive assets. If growth is planned, they are also likely to be investing in additional productive capacity. We can estimate the amount spent on both replacement and additional property, plant and equipment by using the information provided in the financial statements. We can make a crude estimate of capital expenditure by looking at the value of property, plant and equipment at the start of the period, deducting an amount equal to the depreciation written off and comparing it with the value of property, plant and equipment at the end of the period. This will not give us an accurate figure for expenditure on new equipment because the value of a piece of equipment may change between periods (because of revaluation or because it was translated to the home currency at different exchange rates in different periods). It is also possible that the company sold assets during the period; the change between the opening and closing balance will include the book value of any assets sold, but may also reflect gains or losses which must be taken into account.

The company may also have **capitalised interest** already included in the cash flow as an interest expense. Taking all these factors into account, we can make a reasonably accurate estimate of the cash spent by the company on fixed assets:

	OUFS line ref.	£m
Property, plant and equipment at the start of the period	148	223.4
Depreciation for the year	320	(19.4)
Property, plant and equipment at the end of the period	148	(240.0)
Property, plant and equipment revaluation for the year	280	0.0
Foreign exchange translation gain or loss on property, plant and equipment for the year	281	(1.8)
Capitalised interest	339	0.0
Book value of property, plant and equipment sold	278	(8.7)
Expenditure on property, plant and equipment	530	(46.5)

Our estimate of capital expenditure takes into account the possibility that the company sold fixed assets during the period, but ignores any cash received from such sales.

The cash proceeds must be added to the cash flow as an additional source of cash.

The next long-term use of funds we consider is net expenditure on investments. We look first at the change in the value of investments between the start and end of the period. This overstates the cash spent on investments since part of the change during the period arises because the value of the underlying investments changed by an amount equal to the equity income of the company (or the retained earnings of the company). The value of the investments may also have changed during the period because the exchange rate at which the investments were translated has changed. Adjusting for these factors, we can calculate the cash that was spent on investments during the period.

At this stage we add in any sources of cash received by the company which we do not regard as core income. Our derived cash flow makes the prudent assumption that neither interest nor dividends received are core income. This might be an over-conservative assumption for a company such as a retailer offering credit terms to its customers, but appropriate for a company which simply holds excess cash balances.

We now must take into account any investments or accruals associated with other elements on the balance sheet or income statement. For the most part these are small; if they are not, you must pause to think of the cash implications. For example, if provisions increase, you should consider when the provisions are likely to be used. They may not be realised for many years (pension provisions) or they may be used almost immediately (provisions for restructuring or redundancies). If you fail to take into account any changes in intangibles, other long-term assets, other long-term liabilities, provisions, minority interests, reserves, non-core income or exceptional/ extraordinary income or expense your cash flow will not balance.

	OUFS line ref.	£m
Cash flow before long-term uses	529	(20.2)
Expenditure on property, plant and equipment	530	(46.5)
Proceeds from the sale of property, plant and equipment	279	0.5
Net expenditure on investments	333, 343, 349, 153	4.9
Interest received	340	0.0
Dividends received	344	0.0
Change in intangibles	178, 322	0.0
Change in other long-term assets	158, 163, 170–172	(0.3)
Change in other long-term liabilities	249	1.7
Change in provisions	233, 257	0.0
Change in minority interests	258, 361, 362	0.0
Change in reserves	264–268, 280, 281, 367–372	124.5
Other non-core income	331, 333, 341, 342, 346, 347	16.6
Exceptional/extraordinary income or expense	350, 351, 359, 360	(151.0)
Cash flow after investing activities	544	(69.8)

We can now look at how the company chose to finance any cash shortfall after making all its investment decisions, or what it did with any surplus cash. The first source of external funds that we consider is share capital. If we look at the change in the share capital, share premium and preference shares, we can calculate how much cash was raised from equity investors.

Similarly, by looking at the change in long-term debt we can identify how much finance was raised from this source. In calculating inflow or outflow related to long-term debt you should remember that we have already taken into account the obligatory repayment of debt – do not count it twice. We can calculate the use of short-term debt by looking at the change during the period:

	OUFS line ref.	£m
Cash flow after investing activities	544	(69.8)
Change in share capital	260–263, 365	0.1
Change in long-term debt	215, 216, 244	48.4
Change in short-term debt	212–214	5.9
Cash flow after financing activities	548	(15.4)

At this point we have taken into account all sources and uses of cash whether they arose from the company's operations, the sale or purchase of assets, or the increase or reduction of a liability. The cash flow arising from all these elements will coincide with the change in the level of cash balances held by the company. If the cash balance goes down (a source), we know that there must have been a shortfall (or use) after investing activities.

Although the manual calculation of a cash flow is time-consuming, it allows us to learn a great deal about the financial health of a company's operations. The OUFS performs the mechanical calculations for you, but it is worth noting that the key information telling about the immediate prospects for a company's survival is near the top of the cash flow. Provided operating cash flow is sufficient to cover obligatory payments (you must decide whether dividends are obligatory or not) the company is likely to survive. Calculations to that stage of the cash flow fit easily on the back of an envelope! Table 8.1 summarises the logic of the OUFS cash flow.

To summarise, the calculation starts with net operating profit and adds back any non-cash deductions to give the sub-total EBITDA.

Additional sources and uses of cash associated with the company's current operations (for example the build up of inventory or longer credit terms from suppliers) are added back. Any sources or uses from miscellaneous current assets and liabilities are also added back to give operating cash flow.

Cashflow Format.

Table 8.1   The OUFS derived cash flow

Net operating profit

+ Depreciation

EBITDA

+/– Δ Net operating assets

+/– Δ Other current assets

+/– Δ Other current liabilities

Operating cash flow (OCF)

– Taxes paid

– Interest paid

– Current portion long-term debt and leases

Discretionary cash flow

– Dividends paid

Cash flow before long-term uses (CBLTU)

+/– Net expenditure on property, plant and equipment

+/– Net expenditure on investments

+ Non-core income

+/– Δ Other long-term assets

+/– Δ Other long-term liabilities

+/– Exceptional/extraordinary income or expense

Cash flow after investing activities (CFAIA)

+/– Δ Share capital

+/– Δ Long-term debt

+/– Δ Short-term debt

Cash flow after financing activities (CFAFA)

 = Change in cash

Non-discretionary payments – tax, interest and debt repayment – are deducted to give discretionary cash flow.

Dividends paid are deducted to give cash flow before long-term uses.

Investments in fixed assets and other long-term investments and non-core revenues or expenses are added or deducted to give cash flow after investing activities.

Sources or uses of external funding – share capital, long- and short-term debt – are added to give cash flow after financing activities which will be equal in absolute value to the change in the cash on the balance sheet.

8.2   ADJUSTMENTS FOR FORECASTING

The format outlined above is helpful in understanding where the company has raised and spent cash in the past. If we want to use this history to form a basis for forecasts, it is helpful to calculate some adjusted sub-totals.

The first adjusted sub-total to consider is operating free cash flow, which aims to identify the uncommitted cash flows before any financing payments, an important number in calculating the value of a company using discounted cash flow, as we will see in Unit 6. This is approximated by making two deductions from operating cash flow:

(i) a deduction for maintaining plant and equipment

(ii) a deduction for tax.

The cost of maintaining the productive capacity of plant and equipment is seldom disclosed by the company – capital expenditure will include new investment as well as maintenance. The OUFS makes the frequently used assumption that the annual depreciation charge approximates the cost of maintaining existing plant. This assumption is most defensible in a period of low inflation and is an underestimate if prices are rising, but it is often used where any more accurate information is lacking. Tax paid is the second deduction. Bear in mind that the historical level of taxes paid reflects the relative use of debt v. equity as interest is tax deductible whereas dividends are not; using this adjusted sub-total as a basis for forecasts implicitly assumes that this split is maintained.

In Unit 6 we consider somewhat different statements of capital expenditure and of taxes paid, taking into account specific forecasts for capital expenditure and capital structure.

Operating cash flow

– Taxes Paid

– Depreciation (maintenance capital expenditure)

= Operating Free Cash Flow

The next adjustment focuses on free cash flow, or the cash that could be available to pay dividends, cut debt or make acquisitions. It is calculated by deducting interest paid from operating free cash flow, and is of particular interest to bankers considering additional loans to a company.

Operating free cash flow

– Interest paid

= Free cash flow

The cash available for repaying debt, or making acquisitions, after making payments to existing shareholders, may be estimated by deducting dividends from free cash flow to give residual free cash flow. This calculation recognises that most companies need to pay dividends. It is often a negative number, but nevertheless represents a useful sub-total for lenders considering loans to a company which has historically paid dividends.

Free cash flow

– Dividends

= Residual free cash flow

The final adjusted sub-total which is often used in valuations and ratio calculations is net operating profit after tax (NOPAT). NOPAT is calculated as net operating profit – taxes paid. It is used as an approximation of the annual cash generated by the company's operations before any investment in, or sale of, net operating assets. While there is no explicit calculation to reflect the necessary maintenance of plant and equipment, depreciation has already been deducted at the net operating profit level. This means that the use of NOPAT brings the implied assumption that depreciation covers the cash expense of necessary maintenance:

Net operating profit

– Taxes paid

= Net operating profit after tax (NOPAT)

8.3 CASH FLOW RATIOS

After calculating the sources and uses of cash and a range of sub-totals, we are now in the position to calculate a number of ratios which highlight the relative size of cash inflows and cash obligations.

As with financial structure, a whole range of ratios can be calculated depending on the particular perspective of the analyst. In this section we describe a selection of those which are used.

The ratio of NOPAT to interest paid measures how well the interest was covered before any investment in growth and any other discretionary uses. In the medium term, this ratio should be at least 1.0 in a no-growth situation and more than one if the company is growing. If the company's operations do not generate sufficient cash to cover interest and make some contribution to the financing of growth there is significant risk that it will cease to trade. The exception may be in a start-up, or very high growth situation where external cash (in the form of debt or equity) may be raised on the basis of expected future cash flows.

The lenders to a company naturally like to ensure that the company's operations will generate sufficient cash to service their debt, that is pay both interest and repayment when due. They will therefore focus on the ratio:

$$\frac{\text{NOPAT}}{\text{Interest + the current portion of long-term debt and leases (CPLTD\& L)}}$$

If the cash is not sufficient to cover interest and repayment of debt and leases, the lender must depend on some other external source being found to make up any shortfall. Lenders want to know that they will be repaid from the operations of the company. They do not want to find that they are dependent on another lender or investor taking a more optimistic view than they do when they want to stop lending money to the company.

'Great! But can she lay enough golden eggs to service our debt?'

The investors in a company would generally like to ensure that the company's operations will generate enough cash after tax to cover the obligations to lenders (who take precedence) plus their dividends. Investors will therefore focus on:

$$\frac{\text{NOPAT}}{\text{Interest Paid} + (\text{CPLTD\& L}) + \text{dividends}}$$

In the long term the company must generate enough cash to cover these expenses, although in the short term this ratio is often less than 1.0. A ratio of less than 1.0 is fine if growth is expected and external funds are available, but it is also seen in declining companies that are paying out high dividends in order to placate shareholders. The situation should be carefully evaluated if this ratio continues for several periods at a level less than 1.0.

A growing company needs to invest in additional net operating assets to support additional sales. In a growing company it is therefore useful to establish the cash available to cover obligations after this investment has been made. Operating cash flow (OCF) takes into account the net investment in operating assets; taxes paid and depreciation (as an estimate of maintenance capital expenditure) are deducted from this to give the operating free cash flow (OFCF). This numerator is used in three ratios similar to those listed above; the difference is that this numerator is closer to available cash since it takes into account changes in net operating assets such as any increase in uncollected receivables. This is compared to interest expense in the ratio:

$$\frac{\text{OCF - Taxes paid - depreciation}}{\text{Interest expense}}$$

It is compared with total debt obligations in the ratio:

$$\frac{\text{OCF - Taxes paid - depreciation}}{\text{Interest expense} + \text{CPLTD\& L}}$$

Total financing obligations are the focus of the ratio:

$$\frac{\text{OCF - Taxes paid - depreciation}}{\text{Interest expense} + \text{CPLTD\& L} + \text{dividends}}$$

In order to see if the company is investing in new plant and equipment, we can compare the cash invested in plant and equipment with the value of plant which has been written off as depreciation. If the ratio of depreciation to net expenditure on property, plant and equipment is greater than 1.0, the company's pool of plant and equipment is falling; if it is less than 1.0 the pool is growing. (This ratio is distorted if there has been price inflation, but it remains a useful, if crude, indicator of new investment.)

Lenders find it useful to consider how much the company has borrowed relative to its ability to repay that debt. Debt is divided by NOPAT less interest expense to give the number of years it would take the company to generate sufficient cash to repay debt if it did not grow. The ratio is very rough and ready since it does not take into account the reduction in interest expense as debt is repaid. It does none the less provide a more complete picture than the widely used interest cover. Lenders would like a company to be capable of repaying on this basis within the life of its debt. A company borrowing money for ten years should ideally have a 'years to repay' ratio of about ten years – if years to repay is much longer than the life of the debt, lenders must depend on growth or finding other lenders if the debt is to be repaid on schedule.

8.4 INTERPRETING THE CASH FLOW – AN EXAMPLE

In Section 6 we concluded that despite the fact that the Albert Fisher Group plc had recorded profits and a dramatic increase in return on equity, there were grounds for concern. Examining the cash flow we can gain greater insight into the problems and future outlook for the company.

Throughout the five years up to 1996, Albert Fisher produced a significant positive cash flow at the operating cash flow level. However, the cash generated at this level represented a declining percentage of sales, falling from a high of 6.9% to the 1996 level of 3.5%.

After meeting the obligatory payments for taxes, interest and debt repayment (discretionary cash flow), the company had a cash shortfall in two of the previous four years. When dividend payments are deducted (cash flow before long-term uses) Albert Fisher had a shortfall in three of the previous four years.

The cash shortfall means that there were no internally generated funds available to maintain existing assets or to fund any investment in new plant and equipment.

Albert Fisher's policy of paying high dividends in order to reduce shareholder equity and thus increase the return on equity is a practice that has been successfully followed by other organisations. The most recent examples at the time of writing are provided by UK privatised utilities. In contrast to the pattern in Albert Fisher, the reduction in their shareholders' equity has been in the form of a special 'one-off' dividend. In the case of Albert Fisher it appears that they are simply maintaining a constant level of dividend payments in the face of declining profits.

By choosing to maintain this high level of dividends, Albert Fisher had no internally generated funds to maintain existing assets or invest in new plant and equipment. New investment was needed to move to higher value-added products but it had been funded through debt, dramatically increasing the financial risk of Albert Fisher.

The conclusion is confirmed by looking at the cash flow ratios. If we assume that an investment equal to depreciation is needed to maintain plant and equipment and deduct tax, we see that operations did not generate sufficient cash to pay interest and mandatory debt repayments in three of the previous four years (NOPAT/Interest paid + CPLTD&L ranging from 0.60 to 0.87).

Anticipating the future (based on the 1996 figures) for the company, we see that a very dramatic improvement in margins would be needed if Albert Fisher were to maintain the existing level of dividends and repay their very significant debt burden. As Albert Fisher had been seeking improved margins for the previous five years, while reporting steadily declining margins, it required considerable optimism to conclude that they would be successful going forward. It would appear that the debt was unlikely to be repaid through the cash flows coming from the company's operations, so the only alternative would be asset sales. Shareholders were likely to find that dividends fell as banks declined to advance additional funds in the future.

Exercise 8.1 _____

In the years 1994–1996, Blue Circle's operations have generated sufficient cash to cover dividend payments and contribute to long term investment. In 1997 this was not the case, with cash flow showing a shortfall of £15.1m after the payment of dividends (see Appendix 5).

What factors have contributed to this change?

Does this deterioration provide cause for concern?

SUMMARY

In this section we calculated a derived cash flow for Albert Fisher. We then considered the adjustments to the OUFS derived cash flow that would be required to form the basis for forecasting future cash flows. Ratios based on cash flow and providing a financial health check were then reviewed. Finally, Albert Fisher provided an example of the interpretation of the OUFS derived cash flow and associated ratios.

This section provides the techniques that are needed to answer the all-important question, 'Can the company make all payments as they fall due?'. These techniques also provide a history on which we can draw to help forecast a company's future cash flow, a process that is required to assess a trading partner, to assess the creditworthiness of a company, a task that we address in Unit 3, or to value a company, which we look at in Unit 6.

SUMMARY AND CONCLUSIONS

Now that you are familiar with the tools of financial analysis you should be able to:

- understand the purpose, form and function of the main components of an annual report

- monitor the efficiency of a company over time and relative to competitors

- be aware of strategic options and monitor, through financial analysis, the progress a company has made towards achieving its strategic goals

- choose reliable suppliers and customers, or trading partners for your own organisation

ANSWERS TO EXERCISES

Exercise 2.1

A complete version of the OUFS for Blue Circle can be found on CDROM2, file name OUFSBCI.xls. To help you trace individual entries detailed spreading notes are given in Appendix 3.

Exercise 3.1

The UK cement Industry

FACTORS BUILDING PROFITS	FACTORS LIMITING PROFITS
Threat of new entrants	
• very high fixed costs for plant, for maintaining kilns in working order and for specialised storage and distribution vehicles.	• undifferentiated product • simple technology
• high distribution costs because cement is heavy	
• ownership of the quarries which produce the key raw materials, limestone, clay or shale.	
Bargaining power of customers	
• many independent customers	• no switching costs
Bargaining power of suppliers	
• most cement companies own the suppliers of their raw materials	
Threat of substitutes	
• there is no substitute for cement in many building technologies	
Jockeying for position	
• the industry has a small number of large players • the cement industry is subject to wide variations in demand reflecting the economic cycle.	• high exit costs • high fixed costs • when kilns are running at full capacity, additional capacity can be created only in large increments

Summary of the competitive environment

The very high fixed cost for both the manufacture and distribution of cement, together with the limited access to raw materials, serves to discourage new entrants to the UK cement market.

The small number of vertically integrated players, and the many fragmented customers (who regard cement as an important input) ensure that profits will be high when the economy is buoyant.

The high fixed costs, the cost of closing a kiln and the economies of scale in manufacturing provide strong incentives for tacit co-operation among cement manufacturers to break down when the economy is in recession.

The characteristics of this industry suggest that there will be a small number of players, each dominating in one geographical region because of the combination of high fixed costs and high distribution costs. The small number of players and the importance of timely, high quality deliveries of the product ensures that prices and hence profits are high in periods of high demand. The high fixed costs and high exit barriers provide strong incentives for price competition in a recession.

These factors ensure that profits in this industry are very volatile; very high in periods of economic growth and very low in periods of recession, with a relatively small numbers of players.

Exercise 4.1

The inventory levels held by a retailer are likely to vary in the course of the year if they are selling seasonal products. For example, toy and jewellery retailers make most of each year's sales in the few weeks before Christmas, and inventory patterns reflect this sales pattern – high inventory levels in October, November and early December, falling to a minimal level after the end of the January sales. Companies with seasonal sales patterns often choose their year-end to coincide with the seasonal low point, when inventory (and consequently short-term debt, trade creditors and, hence, gearing or leverage) are at their lowest levels.

Fashion/clothing retailers have a seasonal pattern of demand, holding different inventory for each 'fashion' or 'calendar' season. In common with most retailers, Laura Ashley has chosen a seasonal low point, when inventory would be expected to be at a minimum level. The post-Christmas sales inventories should be cleared by the end of January and the spring and summer inventories should not yet be delivered.

If we made the generous assumption that goods are sold evenly throughout the year and the goods to be sold during the spring season had been delivered by 25 January we might expect to find 1/4 of the year's costs (say, 90 days' costs) held as inventory.

Using the days ratio we can calculate what this figure would be:

$$\text{Inventory days} = \frac{\text{Inventory}}{\text{Cost of goods sold}} \times 365$$

$$90 = \frac{\text{Inventory}}{168.9m} \times 365$$

$$\text{Inventory} = \frac{168.9m}{365} \times 90$$

$$\text{Inventory} = £41.6m$$

In fact, the level of inventory, though much better than the very high levels recorded in 1990 and 1993 (see below), is considerably higher than the level that we calculated on the basis of these 'what if' assumptions, and greater than can be logically justified. Moreover, because Laura Ashley sells 'fashion' it is reasonable to suppose that some of this excess inventory was manufactured in previous years and may be obsolete.

Laura Ashley PLC	1990	1991	1992	1993	1994	1995	1996	1997
Inventory days	376	162	193	276	182	147	141	201
Inventory £m	104.8	64.6	57.2	76.4	70.8	64.0	66.6	93.1

The exercise demonstrates that even where we do not know a lot about a company, common sense and an understanding of the ratios can assist us in quickly diagnosing problems.

Exercise 4.2

A complete OUFS for Blue Circle is provided on CD-ROM 2 with the filename OUFSBCI.xls.

Operating efficiency	OUFS Line ref.	31.12.93	31.12.94	30.12.95	31.12.96	31.12.97
Trade creditor days	218*287/313	38.78	39.70	43.23	40.67	36.49
Accrued expenses days	219*287/313	40.30	46.83	45.91	43.32	40.12
Inventory days	125*287/313	75.48	71.07	84.51	76.44	80.13
- raw material days	119*287/313	26.37	29.49	32.19	32.60	36.89
- work in progress days	120*287/313	15.30	10.79	15.27	14.54	11.24
- finished goods days	121*287/313	33.80	30.79	37.04	29.30	32.00
Trade receivable days	117*287/312	63.05	61.15	61.21	55.77	59.66
Net operating assets £m	117+125+136-218-219	301	273	307	267	349
Net operating assets/sales %	426/312	17.92	15.33	17.29	14.71	18.01
Net property, plant & equipment turnover	312/148	1.64	1.81	1.78	1.88	1.59

While cash and marketable securities have fallen, at £363.5m it remains at a level which is hard to justify as an operational requirement. These very high balances hold down both asset turnover and return on assets and thus depress the return to shareholders. It is an issue which institutional shareholders have forced Blue Circle's management to begin to address.

The company's UK properties are valued at their current use value as on 1 January 1979, as determined by the company's own staff. The company has an extensive landbank on the periphery of London and in Kent, which was originally related to the mining of aggregates. Property prices have increased dramatically since 1979 and much of the land has potential for commercial and residential property development. This landbank therefore has significant value which is not quantified in the accounts.

Exercise 5.1

Supermarket chains usually have negative net operating assets because they sell to their many small customers primarily for cash, while they are able to negotiate long payment terms with their suppliers. The more efficient they are in the control of inventories and trade receivables and the longer the credit terms they negotiate with suppliers, the lower current ratio and the greater the absolute value of their negative net operating assets.

Tesco plc 25 Feb. 95		J. Sainsbury plc 9 Mar. 95	
Inventory days	16.29	Inventory days	18.14
Trade receivables days	3.76	Trade receivables days	5.53
Trade creditors days	28.38	Trade creditors days	25.84
Accrued expenses days	4.51	Accrued expenses days	3.39

An examination of the operating efficiency ratios confirms that Tesco plc, with a current ratio of 0.39 (significantly below Sainsbury's), is much more efficient in managing its cycle of production. Both inventory and trade receivables days were shorter than Sainsbury's, while the trade creditor days and accrued expenses days show that they extracted longer credit terms from their suppliers.

The question remains as to whether Tesco's situation is good or bad. The operations are more efficient than the competition, which is clearly good. However, they would be unable to meet their current liabilities through the liquidation of current assets which might be considered bad. This lack of liquidity does not cause concern in practice because we expect both companies to meet their current liabilities through operating revenues rather than the liquidation of assets. When considering whether current liabilities can be met as they fall due it is often more useful to focus on the cash flow.

Exercise 5.2

$$\text{Gearing} = \frac{\text{Debt}}{\text{Shareholders' equity}} \times 100 = \frac{1788.6}{867.7} = 206.1\%$$

$$\text{Debt/equity ratio} = \frac{\text{Debt}}{\text{Debt + shareholders' equity}} = \frac{1788.6}{1788.6+867.7}$$

$$= \frac{1788.6}{2656.3} = 0.67$$

$$\text{Net gearing} = \frac{\text{Debt} - \text{Cash}}{\text{Shareholders' equity}} \times 100 = \frac{1788.6 - 39.0}{867.7}$$

$$= \frac{1749.6}{867.7} = 201.6\%$$

$$\text{Leverage (gross)} = \frac{\text{Total liabilities}}{\text{Shareholders' equity}} = \frac{2505.3}{867.7} = 2.89$$

$$\text{Leverage (tangible)} = \frac{\text{Total liabilities}}{\text{Shareholders' equity} - \text{Intangibles}}$$

$$= \frac{2505.3}{867.7 - 2069.4} = \frac{2505.3}{(1201.7)} = (2.08)$$

$$\text{Leverage (incl. contingents)} = \frac{\text{Total liabilities} + \text{Contingent liabilities}}{\text{Shareholders' equity} - \text{Intangibles}}$$

$$= \frac{2505.3 + 6.2}{(1201.7)} = \frac{2511.5}{(1201.7)} = (2.09)$$

All the solvency ratios describe a high level of financial risk. Leverage (tangible) is useful in highlighting the significance of intangible assets; the value of these intangible assets should be closely examined given that they represent 57.1% of total assets and more than twice the level of shareholders' funds.

The notes to the accounts relating to the valuation of these intangible assets reveal that they were based primarily on the (subjective) fair value of acquisitions as determined by the directors of the company. The accounting policies for intangible assets were as follows:

Accounting Policies – Intangible Fixed Assets

Publishing Rights, Titles and Benefits – In the case of acquired assets, publishing rights, titles and benefits are stated at fair value on acquisition and are carried forward in the balance sheet. Costs of maintaining publishing rights, titles and benefits are charged to the profit and loss account. Assets developed internally are stated at their development cost, net of any revenues during the development period. No amortisation charge is made unless there is a permanent diminution in value as, in the opinion of the directors, these assets do not have a finite economic life. Subject to annual review, any permanent diminution in value is charged to the profit and loss account.

Development Expenditure – Development expenditure relating to specific projects intended for commercial use is carried forward and amortised over the periods expected to benefit therefrom.

Computer Software – Expenditure relating to computer software is carried forward and amortised over its expected useful life.

Exercise 6.1

The Albert Fisher Group plc:

$$\frac{\text{Cost of goods sold} \times 100}{\text{Sales}} = \frac{1463.8 \times 100}{1697.9} = 86.21\%$$

$$\frac{\text{Selling and distribution expenses} \times 100}{\text{Sales}} = \frac{118.7 \times 100}{1697.9} = 6.99\%$$

$$\frac{\text{Net operating profit} \times 100}{\text{Sales}} = \frac{47.6 \times 100}{1697.9} = 2.8\%$$

$$\frac{\text{Net operating profit}}{\text{Interest expense}} = \frac{47.6}{18.4} = 2.59 \text{ times}$$

$$\frac{\text{Tax} \times 100}{\text{Pre-tax profit}} = \frac{10.4 \times 100}{40.1} = 25.94\%$$

$$\frac{\text{Dividends} \times 100}{\text{Net profit after tax}} = \frac{26.8 \times 100}{29.7} = 90.24\%$$

$$\text{Return on equity} = \frac{\text{Net profit after tax} \times 100}{\text{Shareholders' equity}} = \frac{29.7 \times 100}{148.8} = 19.96\%$$

The profitability ratios for the group suggest a satisfactory performance. Indeed, the overall measure of return on equity shows an impressive increase from 3.83% at the end of August 1992 to 19.96% at the end of August 1996. This impressive performance must be judged against the company's stated strategy of 'focusing on added value' by moving from wholesale food distribution to processed food products.

The cost of goods sold has represented an increasing proportion of sales during the past five years, which is inconsistent with the company's objective of moving to higher-margin products. Similarly, selling and distribution expenses have fallen during the period from a high of 10.31% in 1993 to 6.99%, which is consistent with efficiency but perhaps surprising at a time when the company is moving from commodity products to value-added products. Net operating profit/sales percentage fell through the period from a high of 4.36% to a current level of 2.80%, a relatively low level which certainly does not suggest a successful move to higher margin products.

Interest cover, measured as net operating profit/interest expense has remained relatively stable over the period, ranging from 2.37 to 3.62, a satisfactory level.

The effective tax rate has fallen quite dramatically from 58.37% to 25.94%, which is below the UK corporate tax rate. The reason for a tax rate this low should be investigated.

Dividend cover, measured as dividends/net profit after tax shows that the company paid out more than it earned in four of the five years.

To summarise, although the Albert Fisher Group has consistently reported profits after tax, dramatic growth in return on equity, and steadily increasing dividends for the past five years, there is some cause for concern. The stated policy of moving to higher margin products is not reflected in the numbers, dividend payments have exceeded earnings, eroding shareholders' equity. The return on equity has increased only because shareholders' equity is shrinking faster than profit margins.

Exercise 7.1

The Dupont Pyramid is concerned with the return to debt and equity investors. Therefore the profit figure used must be the profit available to *both* debt and equity investors. Net operating profit is calculated *before* interest and dividends have been deducted.

The core ratios are concerned with the return to equity investors only. Therefore the profit figure used must be the profit available to equity investors. Net profits after tax are calculated *after* interest but *before* dividends have been deducted.

Exercise 7.2

A   High street retailer

(Marks and Spencer plc 20.5.96)

The relatively high level of cash and marketable securities compared to trade debtors indicates a retail environment. The reasonably good return on sales hints more to High Street margins than the lower supermarket profit margins.

B   Holding company

(Laura Ashley Holding Company 27.01.96)

The bulk of the assets are investments in the group companies. No trading results.

C   Hotel and casino chain

(Stakis plc 1.10.95)

This could appear like a retail company. However, the dominance of property value in the balance sheet and very low asset turnover hint towards a hotel chain, possibly with excess capacity in its portfolio of sites.

D   Supermarket chain

(J Sainsbury plc 9.3.96)

Very low trade receivables and high trade creditors and inventory is typical of a food retailer. Lower return on sales than the High Street retailer as the bulk of sales are not luxury items.

E   Advertising agency group

(WPP Group plc 31.12.95)

The key to this company profile is the existence of intangibles in the balance sheet. Brand names will have been capitalised and shown as assets in the accounts.

F   Electrical utility

(East Midlands Electricity 31.3.96)

The low return on sales and return on equity (which is regulated) hint at a utility. The relatively high asset leverage supports this, as this low risk industry means companies can afford to raise quite large amounts of debt.

G   Bank

(National Westminster Group 31.12.95)

The unusually high asset leverage, lack of conventional return on sales and dominance of debtors and creditors in the balance sheet indicate a financial institution.

H   Airline

(British Airways 31.3.96)

A high leverage and low asset turnover mean that this industry has very valuable assets funded primarily through debt. The airline industry fund aircraft through leasing arrangements which are generally disclosed on the balance sheet as long term debt.

Exercise 8.1

While sales in 1997 were 6.83% above the level of the previous year, net operating profit fell during the same period. This fall in net operating profit, from £239.4m to £195.4m, reflects a slight decrease in operating margins and a large exceptional charge. The group recorded a loss of £52.1m on the disposal of two UK brick manufacturing companies and a provision for a further £4.0m loss on the disposal of a UK incinerator company (expected to be realised in March 1998).

The cash available from operations was further reduced as a result of the increase in net operating assets associated with the acquisition of St. Mary's Cement Corporation of Canada.

In spite of these significant uses of cash, the rate of growth in dividends was increased, with dividends rising from 13.3 pence per share to 14.5 pence per share, an increase of 9.02%.

Although it is generally a warning signal when companies maintain or increase dividends in the face of declining profitability, there is little cause for concern in this instance. The 'one-off' exceptional items and the investment in net operating assets associated with the St. Mary's acquisition are unlikely to be repeated. The company's dividend policy reflects the Board of Directors' confidence in the underlying profitability of their operations, and is in line with the growth in earnings before exceptional items.

The company's considerable holding of cash and marketable securities of £363.5m ensures that meeting the shortfall of cash from operations will pose no problems.

APPENDIX 1 BLANK OUFS

OPEN UNIVERSITY FINANCIAL SPREADSHEET

Company Name: Date:
Business: Analyst:
Currency: **Millions**
Domicile:

809 **SUMMARY**		31-Dec-94	31-Dec-95	31-Dec-96	31-Dec-97	31-Dec-98
810						
811 **A S S E T S**	Line Reference					
812 Cash. Deposits and Marketable Securities	111+112	0.0	0.0	0.0	0.0	0.0
813 Trade Receivables	117	0.0	0.0	0.0	0.0	0.0
814 Inventory	125	0.0	0.0	0.0	0.0	0.0
815 Other Current Assets	131+135+136+137	0.0	0.0	0.0	0.0	0.0
816 **Current Assets**	138	0.0	0.0	0.0	0.0	0.0
817 Net Property, Plant and Equipment	148	0.0	0.0	0.0	0.0	0.0
818 Investments	153	0.0	0.0	0.0	0.0	0.0
819 Long Term Receivables	158+163	0.0	0.0	0.0	0.0	0.0
820 Other Long Term Assets	169+170:172	0.0	0.0	0.0	0.0	0.0
821 Intangibles	178	0.0	0.0	0.0	0.0	0.0
822 **Non Current Assets**	179	0.0	0.0	0.0	0.0	0.0
823 **TOTAL ASSETS**	181	0.0	0.0	0.0	0.0	0.0
824						
825 **LIABILITIES**						
826 Short Term Debt	217	0.0	0.0	0.0	0.0	0.0
827 Trade Creditors	218	0.0	0.0	0.0	0.0	0.0
828 Accrued Expenses	219	0.0	0.0	0.0	0.0	0.0
829 Other Current Liabilities	220+224:7+233+234	0.0	0.0	0.0	0.0	0.0
830 **Current Liabilities**	235	0.0	0.0	0.0	0.0	0.0
831 Long Term Debt	244	0.0	0.0	0.0	0.0	0.0
832 Other Non Current Liabilities	248+249	0.0	0.0	0.0	0.0	0.0
833 **Total Liabilities**	250	0.0	0.0	0.0	0.0	0.0
834 Deferred Taxation	251	0.0	0.0	0.0	0.0	0.0
835 Long Term Provisions:	257	0.0	0.0	0.0	0.0	0.0
836 Minority Interests	258	0.0	0.0	0.0	0.0	0.0
837 **Total Liabilities and Provisions**	259	0.0	0.0	0.0	0.0	0.0
838 Share Capital	260:263	0.0	0.0	0.0	0.0	0.0
839 Other Reserves	264:268	0.0	0.0	0.0	0.0	0.0
840 Profit and Loss Reserve	269	0.0	0.0	0.0	0.0	0.0
841 **Shareholder's Equity**	270	0.0	0.0	0.0	0.0	0.0
842 **TOTAL LIABILITIES & EQUITY**	272	0.0	0.0	0.0	0.0	0.0
843						
844 **INCOME STATEMENT**						
845 **TOTAL SALES**	312	0.0	0.0	0.0	0.0	0.0
846 Cost of Goods Sold	313	0.0	0.0	0.0	0.0	0.0
847 Selling & Distribution Expenses	314	0.0	0.0	0.0	0.0	0.0
848 Administrative Expense	315	0.0	0.0	0.0	0.0	0.0
849 Other Operating Income/Expenses	316:317	0.0	0.0	0.0	0.0	0.0
850 Exceptional Items	318	0.0	0.0	0.0	0.0	0.0
851 **NET OPERATING PROFIT (NOP)**	336	0.0	0.0	0.0	0.0	0.0
852 Net Interest Expense	337:340	0.0	0.0	0.0	0.0	0.0
853 Other Financial Income/Expense	341:344	0.0	0.0	0.0	0.0	0.0
854 **PROFIT AFTER FINANCIAL ITEMS**	345	0.0	0.0	0.0	0.0	0.0
855 Other Income/Expense	346:349	0.0	0.0	0.0	0.0	0.0
856 Exceptional Income/Expense	350+351	0.0	0.0	0.0	0.0	0.0
857 **PRE TAX PROFIT**	352	0.0	0.0	0.0	0.0	0.0
858 Taxes	353:357	0.0	0.0	0.0	0.0	0.0
859 **NET PROFIT AFTER TAX (NPAT)**	358	0.0	0.0	0.0	0.0	0.0
860 Extraordinary Income/Expense	359+360	0.0	0.0	0.0	0.0	0.0
861 Minority Interest	361	0.0	0.0	0.0	0.0	0.0
862 Dividends	362:365	0.0	0.0	0.0	0.0	0.0
863 **RETAINED PROFIT OR LOSS FOR THE YEAR**	366	0.0	0.0	0.0	0.0	0.0
864						
865 **RATIO SUMMARY**						
866 Return on Equity (NPAT/Equity %)	416	0.00	0.00	0.00	0.00	0.00
867 Return on Sales (NPAT/Sales %)	413	0.00	0.00	0.00	0.00	0.00
868 Asset Turnover (Sales/Total Assets)	414	0.00	0.00	0.00	0.00	0.00
869 Asset Leverage (Total Assets/Equity)	415	0.00	0.00	0.00	0.00	0.00
870 Net Operating Assets/Sales (%)	427	0.00	0.00	0.00	0.00	0.00
871 Current Ratio	433	0.00	0.00	0.00	0.00	0.00
872 Gross Gearing (%)	436	0.00	0.00	0.00	0.00	0.00
873 Leverage (Gross)	438	0.00	0.00	0.00	0.00	0.00
874 Net Operating Profit / Sales (%)	453	0.00	0.00	0.00	0.00	0.00
875 Net Operating Profit/Interest Expense	454	na	na	na	na	na
876 NOP - Taxes Paid (= NOPAT)(Millions)	462	na	0.0	0.0	0.0	0.0
877 NOPAT/Interest Paid + CPLTD & L+ Divs. Paid	465	na	na	na	na	na
878 Operating Free Cash Flow (OFCF)	553	na	0.0	0.0	0.0	0.0
879 OFCF/Int. Paid + CPLTD &L+Divs. Paid	468	na	na	na	na	na
880 Market Capitalisation (Millions)	486	0.0	0.0	0.0	0.0	0.0

OPEN UNIVERSITY FINANCIAL SPREADSHEET

Company Name:			Date:	
Business:			Analyst:	
Currency:	Units: Millions ▼			
Domicile:			Auditor:	

		31-Dec-94	31-Dec-95	31-Dec-96	31-Dec-97	31-Dec-98
110	**ASSETS**					
111	Cash and Deposits					
112	Marketable Securities					
113	Trade Receivables:					
114	-Net Trade Receivables					
115	- Recoverable under Contracts					
116	-Other Trade Receivables					
117	*Sub Total Trade Receivables*	0.0	0.0	0.0	0.0	0.0
118	Inventory:					
119	- Raw Materials					
120	- Work in Progress					
121	- Finished Goods					
122	- Advance Payments to Suppliers					
123	- Progress Payments					
124	- Development Properties					
125	*Sub Total Inventory*	0.0	0.0	0.0	0.0	0.0
126	Tax Receivable:					
127	Tax Receivable:					
128	-ACT Receivable					
129	-Corporation Tax Receivable					
130	-Other Tax Receivable					
131	*Sub Total Tax Receivable*	0.0	0.0	0.0	0.0	0.0
132	Other Receivables					
133	-Due from Related Companies					
134	-Other Receivables					
135	*Sub Total Other Receivables*	0.0	0.0	0.0	0.0	0.0
136	Prepaid Expenses					
137	Sundry Current Assets					
138	**CURRENT ASSETS**	0.0	0.0	0.0	0.0	0.0
139	Net Property, Plant and Equipment:					
140	-Land and Buildings - Freehold					
141	-Long Leasehold					
142	-Short Leasehold					
143	-Plant and Machinery					
144	-Fixtures and Fittings					
145	-Other Fixed Assets (Depreciable)					
146	-Other Fixed Assets (Non Depreciable)					
147	-Construction in Progress					
148	*Sub Total Net Property, Plant and Equipment*	0.0	0.0	0.0	0.0	0.0
149	Investments:					
150	-Related Company					
151	-Other					
152	-Loans to Related Companies					
153	*Sub Total Investments*	0.0	0.0	0.0	0.0	0.0
154	Long Term Trade Receivables:					
155	- Related Companies					
156	-Trade Loans					
157	-Other Trade Receivables					
158	*Sub Total LT Trade Receivables*	0.0	0.0	0.0	0.0	0.0
159	Other Long Term Receivables:					
160	- Related Companies					
161	-Non Trade Loans					
162	-Other LT Receivables					
163	*Sub Total Other LT Receivables*	0.0	0.0	0.0	0.0	0.0
164	Long TermTax Receivable:					
165	-LT ACT Receivable					
166	-LT Corporation Tax Receivable					
167	-Deferred Tax					
168	-Other LT Tax Receivable					
169	*Sub Total Long Term Tax Receivable*	0.0	0.0	0.0	0.0	0.0
170	Prepaid Expenses					
171	Assets held for Sale (ST & LT)					
172	Sundry Non Current Assets					
173	Intangibles :					
174	Goodwill					
175	-Other Amortising					
176	-Other Nonamortising					
177	- Other					
178	*Sub Total Intangibles*	0.0	0.0	0.0	0.0	0.0
179	**NON CURRENT ASSETS**	0.0	0.0	0.0	0.0	0.0
181	**TOTAL ASSETS**	0.0	0.0	0.0	0.0	0.0
183	**NOTES TO THE BALANCE SHEET:**					
184						
185						
186						
187						
188						

OPEN UNIVERSITY FINANCIAL SPREADSHEET

Company Name: Date:
Business: Analyst:
Currency: Millions
Domicile

	LIABILITIES	31-Dec-94	31-Dec-95	31-Dec-96	31-Dec-97	31-Dec-98
210	**LIABILITIES**					
211	Short Term Debt:					
212	- Bank Loans					
213	- Other					
214	-Bills of Exchange Payable					
215	-Current Portion Long Term Debt					
216	-Current Portion Lease Obligations					
217	*Sub Total Short Term Debt*	0.0	0.0	0.0	0.0	0.0
218	Trade Creditors					
219	Accrued Expenses					
220	Customer Prepayments					
221	Taxes Payable:					
222	-Corporation Tax Payable					
223	-Other Taxes Payable					
224	*Sub Total Taxes Payable*	0.0	0.0	0.0	0.0	0.0
225	Dividends Payable					
226	Due to Related Companies					
227	Other Creditors					
228	Current Provisions:					
229	-Acquisition					
230	-Restructuring					
231	-Retirement /Employee Benefits					
232	-Other Provisions					
233	*Sub Total Current Provisions*	0.0	0.0	0.0	0.0	0.0
234	Other Current Liabilities					
235	**CURRENT LIABILITIES**	0.0	0.0	0.0	0.0	0.0
236	Long Term Debt:					
237	-Leases					
238	-Bank Loans					
239	-Bonds and Debentures					
240	-Other Long Term Debt					
241	-Convertible Long Term Debt					
242	-Subordinated Debt					
243	-Redeemable Preference Shares					
244	*Sub Total Long Term Debt*	0.0	0.0	0.0	0.0	0.0
245	Long Term Taxes Payable:					
246	-Corporation Tax Payable					
247	-Other Taxes Payable					
248	*Sub Total Long TermTaxes Payable*	0.0	0.0	0.0	0.0	0.0
249	Sundry Non Current Liabilities					
250	**TOTAL LIABILITIES**	0.0	0.0	0.0	0.0	0.0
251	Deferred Taxation					
252	Long Term Provisions:					
253	-Acquisition					
254	-Restructuring					
255	-Retirement /Employee Benefits					
256	-Other Provisions					
257	*Sub Total Long Term Provisions*	0.0	0.0	0.0	0.0	0.0
258	Minority Interests					
259	**TOTAL LIABILITIES AND PROVISIONS**	0.0	0.0	0.0	0.0	0.0
260	Ordinary Shares					
261	Preference Shares					
262	Share Premium					
263	Other Share Related					
264	Consolidation Differences					
265	Foreign Exchange Reserve					
266	Revaluation Reserve					
267	Other Reserves - Restricted					
268	Other Reserves -Unrestricted					
269	Profit and Loss Reserve					
270	**SHAREHOLDERS' EQUITY**	0.0	0.0	0.0	0.0	0.0
271						
272	**TOTAL LIABILITIES & EQUITY**	0.0	0.0	0.0	0.0	0.0
273	Cross Check	0.0	0.0	0.0	0.0	0.0
275	**ADDITIONAL BALANCE SHEET INFORMATION:**					
276	Contingent Liabilities					
277	Acquisition of Subsidiary net of Cash					
278	Book Value Property, Plant and Equipment Sold (Input Negative)					
279	Proceeds from Sale of Property, Plant and Equipment					
280	Property, Plant and Equipment Revaluation for the year					
281	Foreign Exchange relating to plant					
282	Number of Shares Issued & Outstanding (In Thousands)					
283	Date of Share Price					
284	Share Price					
285	Earnings per Share					
286	Dividends per Share					
287	No. of Days in Accounting Period	365	365	365	365	365

OPEN UNIVERSITY FINANCIAL SPREADSHEET

Company Name:
Business:
Currency: **Millions**
Domicile

Date:
Analyst:

		31-Dec-94	31-Dec-95	31-Dec-96	31-Dec-97	31-Dec-98
310	**INCOME STATEMENT**					
311						
312	**TOTAL SALES**					
313	Cost of Goods Sold					
314	Selling & Distribution Expenses					
315	Administrative Expense					
316	Other Operating Income					
317	Other Operating Expenses					
318	Exceptional Items					
319	*For Information - Included in Operating Profit:*					
320	*Depreciation*	*Manufacturer*					
321		*Trader*					
322	*Amortisation*					
323	*Operating Leases*	*Property*					
324		*Plant & Equipment*					
325		*Other*					
326	*Personnel*					
327	*Advertising*					
328	*Research & Development*					
329	*Wages & salaries*					
330	*Material Expenses*					
331	*Gain/(Loss) Sale of Fixed Asset*					
332	*Gain/(Loss) Sale of Associate*					
333	*Gain/(Loss) Sale of Investment*					
334	*Royalty Income*					
335	*Foreign Exchange*					
336	**NET OPERATING PROFIT (NOP)**	0.0	0.0	0.0	0.0	0.0
337	Interest Expense					
338	Interest Provisions (Non Cash)					
339	(Capitalised Interest)					
340	Interest Income					
341	Other Financial Income					
342	Other Financial Expense					
343	Equity Income - Associates					
344	Dividend Income					
345	**PROFIT AFTER FINANCIAL ITEMS**	0.0	0.0	0.0	0.0	0.0
346	Sundry Income					
347	Sundry Expense					
348	Gain / Loss on Sale of Fixed Assets					
349	Gain / Loss on Sale of Investment					
350	Exceptional Income					
351	Exceptional Expense					
352	**PRE TAX PROFIT**	0.0	0.0	0.0	0.0	0.0
353	Corporation Tax - Domestic					
354	Corporation Tax - Overseas					
355	Deferred Tax					
356	Prior Year Adjustment					
357	Other Tax					
358	**NET PROFIT AFTER TAX (NPAT)**	0.0	0.0	0.0	0.0	0.0
359	Extraordinary Income					
360	Extraordinary Expense					
361	Minority Interest - Share of RE					
362	Minority Interest - Dividends Paid					
363	Dividends - Ordinary					
364	Dividends - Preference					
365	Dividends - Scrip					
366	**RETAINED PROFIT OR LOSS FOR THE FINANCIAL YEAR**	0.0	0.0	0.0	0.0	0.0
367	*Adjustments to*	Prior Year					
368	*Profit & Loss*	Goodwill Written Off					
369	*Reserve:*	Goodwill Written Back					
370		Foreign Exchange Translation					
371		Transfer to/from Reserves					
372		Other					
373	**CHANGE IN PROFIT AND LOSS RESERVE**	0.0	0.0	0.0	0.0	0.0
374	*Other Adjustments*	Prior Year					
375	*to Shareholders'*	Shares Issued					
376	*Equity:*	Share Issue Premium					
377		Shares Issued for Scrip Dividends					
378		Shares Repurchased					
379		Preference Shares Issued					
380		Other Share related					
381		Goodwill Written Off					
382		Goodwill Written Back					
383		Foreign Exchange Translation					
384		Revaluation for the Year					
385		Transfer to/from Reserves					
386		Other					
387	**CHANGE IN SHAREHOLDER'S EQUITY**	0.0	0.0	0.0	0.0	0.0
388	Cross Check	Profit & Loss	na	na	na	na	na
389		Shareholders Equity	na	na	na	na	na

OPEN UNIVERSITY FINANCIAL SPREADSHEET

Company Name:		Date:
Business:		Analyst:
Currency:	Millions	
Domicile:		

410	RATIO ANALYSIS	Line Reference	31-Dec-94	31-Dec-95	31-Dec-96	31-Dec-97	31-Dec-98
411							
412	**CORE RATIOS**						
413	Return on Sales (NPAT/Sales %)	358/312	0.00	0.00	0.00	0.00	0.00
414	Asset Turnover (Sales/Total Assets)	312/181	0.00	0.00	0.00	0.00	0.00
415	Asset Leverage (Total Assets/Equity)	181/270	0.00	0.00	0.00	0.00	0.00
416	Return on Equity (NPAT/Equity %)	358/270	0.00	0.00	0.00	0.00	0.00
417							
418	**OPERATING EFFICIENCY**						
419	Trade Creditor Days	218*287/313	0.00	0.00	0.00	0.00	0.00
420	Accrued Expenses Days	219*287/313	0.00	0.00	0.00	0.00	0.00
421	Inventory Days	125*287/313	0.00	0.00	0.00	0.00	0.00
422	- Raw Materials Days	119*287/313	0.00	0.00	0.00	0.00	0.00
423	- Work in Progress Days	120*287/313	0.00	0.00	0.00 ·	0.00	0.00
424	- Finished Goods Days	121*287/313	0.00	0.00	0.00	0.00	0.00
425	Trade Receivables Days	117*287/312	0.00	0.00	0.00	0.00	0.00
426	Net Operating Assets (Millions)	117+125+136-218-219	0	0	0	0	0
427	Net Operating Assets/Sales (%)	426/312	0.00	0.00	0.00	0.00	0.00
428	Net Property Plant & Equipment T/O(Sales/NetPP&E)	312/148	0.00	0.00	0.00	0.00	0.00
429	Cash & Marketable Securities/Sales (%)	111+112/312	0.00	0.00	0.00	0.00	0.00
430	Cash & Marketable Securities/Current Assets (%)	111+112/138	0.00	0.00	0.00	0.00	0.00
431							
432	**FINANCIAL STRUCTURE**						
433	Current Ratio	138/235	0.00	0.00	0.00	0.00	0.00
434	Quick Ratio	138-125/235	0.00	0.00	0.00	0.00	0.00
435	Working Capital (Millions)	138-235	0	0	0	0	0
436	Gross Gearing (%)	217+244/270	0.00	0.00	0.00	0.00	0.00
437	Net Gearing (%)	217+244-111-112/270	0.00	0.00	0.00	0.00	0.00
438	Leverage (Gross)	250/270	0.00	0.00	0.00	0.00	0.00
439	Leverage (Tangible Inc. Contingents)	250+276/270-178	0.00	0.00	0.00	0.00	0.00
440	Leverage (Tangible)	250/270-178	0.00	0.00	0.00	0.00	0.00
441	Total Liabilities / Market Cap	250/486	0.00	0.00	0.00	0.00	0.00
442	Total Debt(ST +LT)/Total Debt + Equity	217+244/217+244+270	0.00	0.00	0.00	0.00	0.00
443	Capital Employed(Millions)	217+244+248.9+257.8+270	0	0	0	0	0
444	Total Liabilities/Capital Employed	250/443	0.00	0.00	0.00	0.00	0.00
445	Average Debt (Millions)	(217+244)/2	na	na	na	na	na
446	Int.Expense/Average Debt (%)	337/445	na	na	na	na	na
447							
448	**PROFITABILITY**						
449	Sales (Millions)	312	0	0	0	0	0
450	Change in Sales (%)	312	na	na	na	na	na
451	Cost of Goods Sold / Sales (%)	313/312	na	na	na	na	na
452	Selling & Distribution Expense s / Sales (%)	314/312	na	na	na	na	na
453	Net Operating Profit / Sales (%)	336/312	na	na	na	na	na
454	Net Operating Profit/Interest Expense	336/337	na	na	na	na	na
455	Pre-Tax Profit / Sales (%)	352/312	na	na	na	na	na
456	Effective Tax Rate (%)	353..357/352	na	na	na	na	na
457	Net Profit after Tax / Sales (%)	358/312	na	na	na	na	na
458	Dividends/Net Profit after Tax (%)	362..365/358	na	na	na	na	na
459							
460	**CASHFLOW RATIOS**						
461	EBITDA / Sales (%)	514/312	na	0.0	0.0	0.0	0.0
462	NOP - Taxes Paid (= NOPAT)(Millions)	512 - 524	na	0	0	0	0
463	NOPAT/Interest Paid	462/525	na	na	na	na	na
464	NOPAT/Interest Paid + CPLTD & L	462/(525+526)	na	na	na	na	na
465	NOPAT/Interest Paid + CPLTD & L+ Divs. Paid	462/(525+526+528)	na	na	na	na	na
466	Operating Free Cash Flow(OFCF)/Interest Paid	553/525	na	na	na	na	na
467	OFCF/Int. Paid + CPLTD &L	553/(525+526)	na	na	na	na	na
468	OFCF/Int. Paid + CPLTD &L+Divs. Paid	553/(525+526+528)	na	na	na	na	na
469	Net Expenditure Property, Plant & Equipment (Millions)	532	na	0	0	0	0
470	Net Expenditure PP&E/Total Assets (%)	469/181	na	0.00	0.00	0.00	0.00
471	Net Expenditure PP&E/Sales %	469/312	na	0.00	0.00	0.00	0.00
472	Depn./Net Expenditure PP&E	(320+321)/469	na	0.00	0.00	0.00	0.00
473	Depreciation/Net PP&E (%)	(320+321)/148	na	0.00	0.00	0.00	0.00
474	Years to Repay Debt (Debt/NOPAT-Int. Paid)	(217+244)/(462-525)	na	0.00	0.00	0.00	0.00
475							
476							
477	**MARKET RELATED DATA**						
478	Number of Shares Issued & Outstanding(In Thousands)	282	0	0	0	0	0
479	Date of Share Price	283	0	0	0	0	0
480	Share Price	284	0.00	0.00	0.00	0.00	0.00
481	Earnings per Share	285	0.000	0.000	0.000	0.000	0.000
482	Dividend per Share	286	0.000	0.000	0.000	0.000	0.000
483	Change in Dividend per Share (%)	482	na	na	na	na	na
484	Number of Days in Period Days	287	365	365	365	365	365
485	Discretionary Cash Flow per Share	527/478	na	0.00	0.00	0.00	0.00
486	Market Capitalisation (Millions)	478*480	0	0	0	0	0
487	Price / EBITDA per Share	480/514/478	na	0.0	0.0	0.0	0.0
488	Price / Discretionary Cash Flow per Share	480/527/478	na	0.0	0.0	0.0	0.0
489	Price / Free Cash Flow per Share	480/554/478	na	0.0	0.0	0.0	0.0
490	Price / Book	480/270/478					

OPEN UNIVERSITY FINANCIAL SPREADSHEET

Company Name:				Date:	
Business:				Analyst:	
Currency:	Millions				
Domicile					

	DERIVED CASH FLOW	Line Reference	31-Dec-95	31-Dec-96	31-Dec-97	31-Dec-98
510						
511						
512	NET OPERATING PROFIT (NOP)	336	0.0	0.0	0.0	0.0
513	+ Depreciation / Amortisation	320;321;322	0.0	0.0	0.0	0.0
514	EARNINGS BEFORE INTEREST, TAX, DEP'N & AMORT.(EBITDA)		0.0	0.0	0.0	0.0
515	+/- Δ Trade Receivables	117	0.0	0.0	0.0	0.0
516	+/- Δ Inventory	125	0.0	0.0	0.0	0.0
517	+/- Δ Trade Creditors	218	0.0	0.0	0.0	0.0
518	+/- Δ Accrued Expenses	219	0.0	0.0	0.0	0.0
519	+/- Δ Prepaid Expenses	136	0.0	0.0	0.0	0.0
520	*Sub Total: Change Net Operating Assets*		0.0	0.0	0.0	0.0
521	+/- Δ Other Current Assets	137, 135	0.0	0.0	0.0	0.0
522	+/- Δ Other Current Liabilities	220,226,227,234	0.0	0.0	0.0	0.0
523	OPERATING CASH FLOW (OCF)		0.0	0.0	0.0	0.0
524	- Taxes Paid	224,248,251,353..57,131,169	0.0	0.0	0.0	0.0
525	- Interest Paid	337,338	0.0	0.0	0.0	0.0
526	- Current Portion Long Term Debt & Leases	215,216	0.0	0.0	0.0	0.0
527	DISCRETIONARY CASH FLOW		0.0	0.0	0.0	0.0
528	- Dividends Paid	225,362...365	0.0	0.0	0.0	0.0
529	CASH FLOW BEFORE LONG TERM USES (CFBLTU)		0.0	0.0	0.0	0.0
530	- Expenditure on Property, Plant and Equipment	148,320,321,348,339,278,280,281	0.0	0.0	0.0	0.0
531	+ Proceeds from Sale of Property, Plant & Equip.	279	0.0	0.0	0.0	0.0
532	*Subtotal Net Expenditure on PP&E*		0.0	0.0	0.0	0.0
533	+/- Net Expenditure on Investments	333,343,349,153	0.0	0.0	0.0	0.0
534	+ Interest Received	340	0.0	0.0	0.0	0.0
535	+ Dividends Received	344	0.0	0.0	0.0	0.0
536	+/- Δ Intangibles	178,322	0.0	0.0	0.0	0.0
537	+/- Δ Other Long Term Assets	158,163,170,171,172	0.0	0.0	0.0	0.0
538	+/- Δ Other Long Term Liabilities	249	0.0	0.0	0.0	0.0
539	+/- Δ Provisions	233,257	0.0	0.0	0.0	0.0
540	+/- Δ Minority Interests	258,361,362	0.0	0.0	0.0	0.0
541	+/- Δ Reserves	264..268,280,281,367..372	0.0	0.0	0.0	0.0
542	+ Other Non-core Income	331,333,341,342,346,347	0.0	0.0	0.0	0.0
543	+/- Exceptional / Extraordinary Inome or Expense	350,351,359,360	0.0	0.0	0.0	0.0
544	CASH FLOW AFTER INVESTING ACTIVITIES (CFAIA)		0.0	0.0	0.0	0.0
545	+/- Δ Share Capital	260..263,365	0.0	0.0	0.0	0.0
546	+/- Δ Long Term Debt	215,216,244	0.0	0.0	0.0	0.0
547	+/- Δ Short Term Debt	212..214	0.0	0.0	0.0	0.0
548	CASH FLOW AFTER FINANCING ACTIVITIES (CFAFA)		0.0	0.0	0.0	0.0
549	CHANGE IN CASH	111,112	0.0	0.0	0.0	0.0
550			0.0	0.0	0.0	0.0
551	**Adjusted Cash Flow Subtotals:**					
553	Operating Free Cash Flow (OFCF)	523-513+524	0.0	0.0	0.0	0.0
554	Free Cash Flow (FCF)	553+525	0.0	0.0	0.0	0.0
555	Residual Free Cash Flow (RFCF)	554+528	0.0	0.0	0.0	0.0
556	Adjusted Operating Cash Flow (AOCF)	514+520	0.0	0.0	0.0	0.0

OPEN UNIVERSITY FINANCIAL SPREADSHEET

Company Name:		Date:
Business:		Analyst:
Currency:	Millions	
Domicile:		

	BREAKDOWN BY DIVISION	31-Dec-94	31-Dec-95	31-Dec-96	31-Dec-97	31-Dec-98
610	**BREAKDOWN BY DIVISION**					
611	**SALES BY DIVISION**					
612	Division 1					
613	Division 2					
614	Division 3					
615	Division 4					
616	Division 5					
617	Subtotal Continuing Operations	0.0	0.0	0.0	0.0	0.0
618	Discontinued Operations					
619	Other					
620	Other					
621	**TOTAL**	0.0	0.0	0.0	0.0	0.0
622	**% CHANGE IN SALES**					
623	Division 1					
624	Division 2					
625	Division 3					
626	Division 4					
627	Division 5					
628	Subtotal Continuing Operations					
629	Discontinued Operations					
630	Other					
631	Other					
632	**TOTAL**					
633	**SALES BY DIVISION AS % OF TOTAL SALES**					
634	Division 1					
635	Division 2					
636	Division 3					
637	Division 4					
638	Division 5					
639	Subtotal Continuing Operations					
640	Discontinued Operations					
641	Other					
642	Other					
643	**TOTAL**					
644	**NET OPERATING PROFIT BY DIVISION**					
645	Division 1					
646	Division 2					
647	Division 3					
648	Division 4					
649	Division 5					
650	Subtotal Continuing Operations	0.0	0.0	0.0	0.0	0.0
651	Discontinued Operations					
652	Other					
653	Other					
654	**TOTAL**	0.0	0.0	0.0	0.0	0.0
655	**% CHANGE IN NET OPERATING PROFIT BY DIVISION**					
656	Division 1					
657	Division 2					
658	Division 3					
659	Division 4					
660	Division 5					
661	Subtotal Continuing Operations					
662	Discontinued Operations					
663	Other					
664	Other					
665	**TOTAL**					
666	**NET OPERATING PROFIT % OF SALES BY DIVISION**					
667	Division 1					
668	Division 2					
669	Division 3					
670	Division 4					
671	Division 5					
672	Subtotal Continuing Operations					
673	Discontinued Operations					
674	Other					
675	Other					
676	**TOTAL**					

OPEN UNIVERSITY FINANCIAL SPREADSHEET

Company Name:				Date:	
Business:				Analyst:	
Currency:	Millions				
Domicile:					

	BREAKDOWN BY AREA	31-Dec-94	31-Dec-95	31-Dec-96	31-Dec-97	31-Dec-98
710	**BREAKDOWN BY AREA**					
711	**SALES BY AREA**					
712	Area 1					
713	Area 2					
714	Area 3					
715	Area 4					
716	Area 5					
717	Subtotal Continuing Operations	0.0	0.0	0.0	0.0	0.0
718	Discontinued Operations					
719	Other					
720	Other					
721	**TOTAL**	0.0	0.0	0.0	0.0	0.0
722	**% CHANGE IN SALES**					
723	Area 1					
724	Area 2					
725	Area 3					
726	Area 4					
727	Area 5					
728	Subtotal Continuing Operations					
729	Discontinued Operations					
730	Other					
731	Other					
732	**TOTAL**					
733	**SALES BY AREA AS % OF TOTAL SALES**					
734	Area 1					
735	Area 2					
736	Area 3					
737	Area 4					
738	Area 5					
739	Subtotal Continuing Operations					
740	Discontinued Operations					
741	Other					
742	Other					
743	**TOTAL**					
744	**NET OPERATING PROFIT BY AREA**					
745	Area 1					
746	Area 2					
747	Area 3					
748	Area 4					
749	Area 5					
750	Subtotal Continuing Operations	0.0	0.0	0.0	0.0	0.0
751	Discontinued Operations					
752	Other					
753	Other					
754	**TOTAL**	0.0	0.0	0.0	0.0	0.0
755	**% CHANGE IN NET OPERATING PROFIT BY AREA**					
756	Area 1					
757	Area 2					
758	Area 3					
759	Area 4					
760	Area 5					
761	Subtotal Continuing Operations					
762	Discontinued Operations					
763	Other					
764	Other					
765	**TOTAL**					
766	**NET OPERATING PROFIT % OF SALES BY AREA**					
767	Area 1					
768	Area 2					
769	Area 3					
770	Area 4					
771	Area 5					
772	Subtotal Continuing Operations					
773	Discontinued Operations					
774	Other					
775	Other					
776	**TOTAL**					

APPENDIX 2   BLUE CIRCLE OUFS

OPEN UNIVERSITY FINANCIAL SPREADSHEET

Company Name:	Blue Circle Industries PLC		Date: 12-Jun-98
Business:	Building Mat'ls & Property Dev't		Analyst: PAS
Currency:	Sterling	Units: Millions	
Domicile:	UK		Auditor: Ernst & Young

	ASSETS	31-Dec-93	31-Dec-94	31-Dec-95	31-Dec-96	31-Dec-97
111	Cash and Deposits	26.6	35.1	55.8	40.9	45.9
112	Marketable Securities	360.5	475.9	567.6	488.2	317.6
113	Trade Receivables:					
114	-Net Trade Receivables	290.0	298.2	297.6	277.3	316.9
115	- Recoverable under Contracts					
116	-Other Trade Receivables					
117	*Sub Total Trade Receivables*	290.0	298.2	297.6	277.3	316.9
118	Inventory:					
119	- Raw Materials	84.8	97.6	103.5	105.8	129.9
120	- Work in Progress	49.2	35.7	49.1	47.2	39.6
121	- Finished Goods	108.7	101.9	119.1	95.1	112.7
122	- Advance Payments to Suppliers					
123	- Progress Payments					
124	- Development Properties					
125	*Sub Total Inventory*	242.7	235.2	271.7	248.1	282.2
127	Tax Receivable:					
128	-ACT Receivable	14.5	16.7	21.7	18.2	39.3
129	-Corporation Tax Receivable					
130	-Other Tax Receivable					
131	*Sub Total Tax Receivable*	14.5	16.7	21.7	18.2	39.3
132	Other Receivables					
133	-Due from Related Companies	1.7	2.5	2.6	3.0	6.5
134	-Other Receivables	22.7	24.7	45.6	39.1	30.3
135	*Sub Total Other Receivables*	24.4	27.2	48.2	42.1	36.8
136	Prepaid Expenses	22.4	25.8	24.1	14.1	19.9
137	Sundry Current Assets					
138	CURRENT ASSETS	981.1	1,114.1	1,286.7	1,128.9	1,058.6
139	Net Property, Plant and Equipment:					
140	-Land and Buildings - Freehold	433.7	408.6	409.8	370.9	393.0
141	-Long Leasehold	2.8	3.0	3.1	3.1	3.3
142	-Short Leasehold	2.8	2.9	3.2	3.0	1.3
143	-Plant and Machinery	556.6	523.2	535.4	526.4	708.3
144	-Fixtures and Fittings					
145	-Other Fixed Assets (Depreciable)					
146	-Other Fixed Assets (Non Depreciable)					
147	-Construction in Progress	27.9	44.9	45.0	63.0	115.9
148	*Sub Total Net Property, Plant and Equipment*	1,023.8	982.6	996.5	966.4	1,221.8
149	Investments:					
150	-Related Company	176.1	183.0	188.7	216.3	183.0
151	-Other	1.6	0.3	0.3	2.0	9.9
152	-Loans to Related Companies	4.5	4.5	4.5	28.3	18.3
153	*Sub Total Investments*	182.2	187.8	193.5	246.6	211.2
154	Long Term Trade Receivables:					
155	- Related Companies					
156	-Trade Loans					
157	-Other Trade Receivables	7.2	15.5	10.0	4.2	2.5
158	*Sub Total LT Trade Receivables*	7.2	15.5	10.0	4.2	2.5
159	Other Long Term Receivables:					
160	- Related Companies					
161	-Non Trade Loans					
162	-Other LT Receivables	1.6	2.2	2.5	1.7	13.2
163	*Sub Total Other LT Receivables*	1.6	2.2	2.5	1.7	13.2
164	Long TermTax Receivable:					
165	-LT ACT Receivable	12.4	19.7	4.7	11.0	7.5
166	-LT Corporation Tax Receivable					
167	-Deferred Tax					
168	-Other LT Tax Receivable					
169	*Sub Total Long Term Tax Receivable*	12.4	19.7	4.7	11.0	7.5
170	Prepaid Expenses	42.8	50.1	55.0	67.3	78.1
171	Assets held for Sale (ST & LT)					
172	Sundry Non Current Assets					
173	Intangibles :					
174	Goodwill					
175	-Other Amortising					
176	-Other Nonamortising					
177	- Other					
178	*Sub Total Intangibles*	0.0	0.0	0.0	0.0	0.0
179	NON CURRENT ASSETS	1,270.0	1,257.9	1,262.2	1,297.2	1,534.3
181	TOTAL ASSETS	2,251.1	2,372.0	2,548.9	2,426.1	2,592.9

183   NOTES TO THE BALANCE SHEET:
184
185
186
187
188

OPEN UNIVERSITY FINANCIAL SPREADSHEET

Company Name: Blue Circle Industries PLC
Business: Building Mat'ls & Property Dev't
Currency: Sterling Millions
Domicile UK

Date: 12-Jun-98
Analyst: PAS

	LIABILITIES	31-Dec-93	31-Dec-94	31-Dec-95	31-Dec-96	31-Dec-97
210						
211	Short Term Debt:					
212	- Bank Loans	217.5	328.0	336.5	249.2	253.6
213	- Other					
214	-Bills of Exchange Payable					
215	-Current Portion Long Term Debt	93.0	3.0	1.6	1.3	5.3
216	-Current Portion Lease Obligations	1.8	0.1	0.1	0.5	0.1
217	*Sub Total Short Term Debt*	312.3	331.1	338.2	251.0	259.0
218	Trade Creditors	124.7	131.4	139.0	132.0	128.9
219	Accrued Expenses	129.6	155.0	147.6	140.6	141.3
220	Customer Prepayments					
221	Taxes Payable:					
222	-Corporation Tax Payable	47.0	62.2	70.5	67.1	71.6
223	-Other Taxes Payable					
224	*Sub Total Taxes Payable*	47.0	62.2	70.5	67.1	71.6
225	Dividends Payable	51.8	58.3	62.3	66.6	74.7
226	Due to Related Companies	0.5	0.5	0.5	0.5	1.1
227	Other Creditors	43.5	49.8	57.4	55.3	46.4
228	Current Provisions:					
229	-Acquisition					
230	-Restructuring					
231	-Retirement /Employee Benefits					
232	-Other Provisions					
233	*Sub Total Current Provisions*	0.0	0.0	0.0	0.0	0.0
234	Other Current Liabilities					
235	**CURRENT LIABILITIES**	709.4	788.3	815.5	713.1	722.6
236	Long Term Debt:					
237	-Leases	1.8	0.6	0.7	0.6	0.7
238	-Bank Loans	150.1	30.2	53.1	19.7	45.3
239	-Bonds and Debentures	280.1	273.2	266.4	257.7	301.8
240	-Other Long Term Debt					
241	-Convertible Long Term Debt					
242	-Subordinated Debt	3.1	2.4	1.4	1.3	1.2
243	-Redeemable Preference Shares					
244	*Sub Total Long Term Debt*	435.1	306.4	321.6	279.3	349.0
245	Long Term Taxes Payable:					
246	-Corporation Tax Payable	0.3	13.2	13.4	27.6	64.5
247	-Other Taxes Payable					
248	*Sub Total Long TermTaxes Payable*	0.3	13.2	13.4	27.6	54.5
249	Sundry Non Current Liabilities	37.7	64.6	74.5	80.1	96.4
250	**TOTAL LIABILITIES**	1,182.5	1,172.5	1,225.0	1,100.1	1,222.5
251	Deferred Taxation	17.2	21.6	21.3	23.9	40.8
252	Long Term Provisions:					
253	-Acquisition					
254	-Restructuring	23.9	13.1	67.2	26.8	36.4
255	-Retirement /Employee Benefits					
256	-Other Provisions					
257	*Sub Total Long Term Provisions*	23.9	13.1	67.2	26.8	36.4
258	Minority Interests	46.9	52.2	60.6	63.9	50.8
259	**TOTAL LIABILITIES AND PROVISIONS**	1,270.5	1,259.4	1,374.1	1,214.7	1,350.5
260	Ordinary Shares	345.9	364.3	366.5	369.7	378.6
261	Preference Shares	107.1	107.1	106.8	101.5	80.6
262	Share Premium	264.8	269.2	276.0	287.7	399.8
263	Other Share Related					
264	Consolidation Differences					
265	Foreign Exchange Reserve					
266	Revaluation Reserve	46.9	44.0	40.8	37.3	36.1
267	Other Reserves - Restricted		72.2	72.2	72.2	
268	Other Reserves -Unrestricted	80.1	84.2	88.5	96.0	92.4
269	Profit and Loss Reserve	135.8	171.6	224.0	247.0	254.9
270	**SHAREHOLDERS' EQUITY**	980.6	1,112.6	1,174.8	1,211.4	1,242.4
271						
272	**TOTAL LIABILITIES & EQUITY**	2,251.1	2,372.0	2,548.9	2,426.1	2,592.9
273	Cross Check	0.0	0.0	0.0	0.0	0.0
275	**ADDITIONAL BALANCE SHEET INFORMATION:**					
276	Contingent Liabilities	11.7	5.6	5.3	6.2	3.0
277	Acquisition of Subsidiary net of Cash	0.0	0.0	(4.0)	(3.2)	(167.0)
278	Book Value Property, Plant and Equipment Sold (Input Negative)	(16.4)	(33.9)	(26.0)	(31.7)	(32.2)
279	Proceeds from Sale of Property, Plant and Equipment	14.7	41.3	20.8	22.4	27.1
280	Property, Plant and Equipment Revaluation for the year	14.4	12.6	13.3	10.7	6.7
281	Foreign Exchange relating to plant	(14.2)	(17.8)	2.6	60.3	18.1
282	Number of Shares Issued & Outstanding (In Thousands)	691,804.0	728,500.0	723,900.0	739,400.0	757,200.0
283	Date of Share Price	Year High	Year High	Year High	Year High	Year High
284	Share Price	3.58	3.87	3.42	4.14	4.49
285	Earnings per Share	0.145	0.127	0.184	0.235	0.170
286	Dividends per Share	0.113	0.118	0.125	0.133	0.145
287	No. of Days in Accounting Period	365	365	365	365	365

OPEN UNIVERSITY FINANCIAL SPREADSHEET

Company Name:	Blue Circle Industries PLC	Date: 12-Jun-98
Business:	Building Mat'ls & Property Dev't	Analyst: PAS
Currency:	Sterling Millions	
Domicile	UK	

	INCOME STATEMENT	31-Dec-93	31-Dec-94	31-Dec-95	31-Dec-96	31-Dec-97
310						
311						
312	**TOTAL SALES**	1,678.8	1,779.8	1,774.6	1,814.8	1,938.8
313	Cost of Goods Sold	(1,173.7)	(1,208.0)	(1,173.5)	(1,184.7)	(1,285.4)
314	Selling & Distribution Expenses	(247.7)	(255.4)	(274.7)	(286.3)	(305.1)
315	Administrative Expense	(107.1)	(115.0)	(115.1)	(109.1)	(109.4)
316	Other Operating Income	7.7	10.7	12.6	4.7	12.6
317	Other Operating Expenses					
318	Exceptional Items		(16.2)	(8.3)		(56.1)
319	*For Information - Included in Operating Profit:*					
320	*Depreciation Manufacturer*	*(95.6)*	*(91.8)*	*(95.2)*	*(94.0)*	*(106.8)*
321	*Trader*					
322	*Amortisation*					
323	*Operating Leases Property*					
324	*Plant & Equipment*	*(3.7)*	*(4.2)*	*(5.2)*	*(7.2)*	*(10.5)*
325	*Other*	*(6.3)*	*(5.0)*	*(4.7)*	*(3.5)*	*(3.8)*
326	*Personnel*					
327	*Advertising*					
328	*Research & Development*	*(12.9)*	*(12.8)*	*(11.8)*	*(10.6)*	*(5.0)*
329	*Wages & salaries*	*(371.0)*	*(390.1)*	*(407.9)*	*(404.4)*	*(420.0)*
330	*Material Expenses*					
331	*Gain/(Loss) Sale of Fixed Asset*	*(1.7)*	*7.4*	*(5.2)*	*(9.3)*	*(5.1)*
332	*Gain/(Loss) Sale of Associate*					
333	*Gain/(Loss) Sale of Investment*					
334	*Royalty Income*					
335	*Foreign Exchange*					
336	**NET OPERATING PROFIT (NOP)**	158.0	195.9	215.6	239.4	195.4
337	Interest Expense	(65.1)	(51.8)	(55.2)	(47.0)	(54.2)
338	Interest Provisions (Non Cash)					
339	(Capitalised Interest)					
340	Interest Income	32.3	30.9	41.7	39.7	43.2
341	Other Financial Income					
342	Other Financial Expense					
343	Equity Income - Associates	18.1	31.7	33.7	40.1	30.6
344	Dividend Income	22.3	20.9	28.7	25.4	31.3
345	**PROFIT AFTER FINANCIAL ITEMS**	165.6	227.6	264.5	297.6	246.3
346	Sundry Income					
347	Sundry Expense					
348	Gain / Loss on Sale of Fixed Assets					
349	Gain / Loss on Sale of Investment					
350	Exceptional Income		4.0	54.3		
351	Exceptional Expense		(47.2)	(55.0)		
352	**PRE TAX PROFIT**	165.6	184.4	263.8	297.6	246.3
353	Corporation Tax - Domestic	(18.0)	(39.0)	(64.2)	(62.5)	(55.7)
354	Corporation Tax - Overseas	(25.7)	(27.2)	(40.8)	(48.2)	(50.9)
355	Deferred Tax	(10.3)	(10.1)	(14.0)	(7.6)	0.2
356	Prior Year Adjustment	1.3	1.8	2.5	(0.2)	0.3
357	Other Tax	0.7	(2.6)	8.9	19.4	7.8
358	**NET PROFIT AFTER TAX (NPAT)**	113.6	107.3	156.2	198.5	148.0
359	Extraordinary Income					
360	Extraordinary Expense					
361	Minority Interest - Share of RE	(5.6)	(8.1)	(13.7)	(17.7)	(14.0)
362	Minority Interest - Dividends Paid					
363	Dividends - Ordinary	(77.7)	(87.6)	(91.7)	(98.0)	(109.6)
364	Dividends - Preference	(8.2)	(8.2)	(8.2)	(7.9)	(6.9)
365	Dividends - Scrip					
366	**RETAINED PROFIT OR LOSS FOR THE FINANCIAL YEAR**	22.1	3.4	42.6	74.9	17.5
367	*Adjustments to* Prior Year					
368	*Profit & Loss* Goodwill Written Off				(4.2)	
369	*Reserve:* Goodwill Written Back	0.3	36.8			50.8
370	Foreign Exchange Translation	(17.0)	2.1	9.4	(40.2)	(43.3)
371	Transfer to/from Reserves	2.9	(6.5)	0.4	(7.5)	(17.1)
372	Other					
373	**CHANGE IN PROFIT AND LOSS RESERVE**	8.3	35.8	52.4	23.0	7.9
374	*Other Adjustments* Prior Year					
375	*to Shareholders'* Shares Issued	2.3	18.4	1.9	3.2	8.9
376	*Equity:* Share Issue Premium	7.4	4.4	6.8	11.7	112.1
377	Shares Issued for Scrip Dividends					
378	Shares Repurchased					
379	Preference Shares Issued	(0.1)			(5.3)	(20.9)
380	Other Share related		72.2			
381	Goodwill Written Off					
382	Goodwill Written Back					
383	Foreign Exchange Translation	(5.2)	(11.5)	(6.0)	(9.2)	(17.9)
384	Revaluation for the Year	8.7	7.4	7.5	5.7	(1.2)
385	Transfer to/from Reserves	(4.1)	5.3	(0.4)	7.5	(57.9)
386	Other					
387	**CHANGE IN SHAREHOLDER'S EQUITY**	17.3	132.0	62.2	36.6	31.0
388	Cross Check Profit & Loss	na	0.0	0.0	0.0	0.0
389	Shareholders Equity	na	0.0	0.0	0.0	0.0

OPEN UNIVERSITY FINANCIAL SPREADSHEET

Company Name:	Blue Circle Industries PLC
Business:	Building Mat'ls & Property Dev't
Currency:	Sterling Millions
Domicile:	UK

Date: 12-Jun-98
Analyst: PAS

	BREAKDOWN BY DIVISION	31-Dec-93	31-Dec-94	31-Dec-95	31-Dec-96	31-Dec-97
610	**SALES BY DIVISION**					
611						
612	Division 1-Heavy Building Materials	826.7	876.4	928.8	966.5	1,166.8
613	Division 2-Heating (Home Products to 1994)	821.5	823.6	655.0	640.3	575.5
614	Division 3-Bathrooms			172.4	175.2	174.0
615	Division 4-Property	24.1	72.3	17.0	30.8	21.0
616	Division 5-Other	6.5	7.5	1.4	2.0	1.5
617	Subtotal Continuing Operations	1,678.8	1,779.8	1,774.6	1,814.8	1,938.8
618	Discontinued Operations					
619	Other-Related Companies	252.0	282.3	302.1	344.8	380.4
620	Other					
621	**TOTAL**	1,930.8	2,062.1	2,076.7	2,159.6	2,319.2
622	**% CHANGE IN SALES**					
623	Division 1-Heavy Building Materials		6.01%	5.98%	4.06%	20.72%
624	Division 2-Heating (Home Products to 1994)		0.26%	(20.47%)	(2.24%)	(10.12%)
625	Division 3-Bathrooms				1.62%	(0.68%)
626	Division 4-Property		200.00%	(76.49%)	81.18%	(31.82%)
627	Division 5-Other		15.38%	(81.33%)	42.86%	(25.00%)
628	Subtotal Continuing Operations		6.02%	(0.29%)	2.27%	6.83%
629	Discontinued Operations					
630	Other-Related Companies		12.02%	7.01%	14.13%	10.32%
631	Other					
632	**TOTAL**		6.80%	0.71%	3.99%	7.39%
633	**SALES BY DIVISION AS % OF TOTAL SALES**					
634	Division 1-Heavy Building Materials	42.82%	42.50%	44.72%	44.75%	50.31%
635	Division 2-Heating (Home Products to 1994)	42.55%	39.94%	31.54%	29.65%	24.81%
636	Division 3-Bathrooms			8.30%	8.11%	7.50%
637	Division 4-Property	1.25%	3.51%	0.82%	1.43%	0.91%
638	Division 5-Other	0.34%	0.36%	0.07%	0.09%	0.06%
639	Subtotal Continuing Operations	86.95%	86.31%	85.45%	84.03%	83.60%
640	Discontinued Operations					
641	Other-Related Companies	13.05%	13.69%	14.55%	15.97%	16.40%
642	Other					
643	**TOTAL**	100.00%	100.00%	100.00%	100.00%	100.00%
644	**NET OPERATING PROFIT BY DIVISION**					
645	Division 1-Heavy Building Materials	98.1	145.2	180.7	178.9	226.4
646	Division 2-Heating (Home Products to 1994)	64.4	67.1	17.1	35.0	50.0
647	Division 3-Bathrooms			27.0	24.6	24.6
648	Division 4-Property	5.1	11.0	3.3	11.9	173
649	Division 5-Other	(9.6)	(11.2)	(4.2)	(10.9)	(11.2)
650	Subtotal Continuing Operations	158.0	212.1	223.9	239.5	291.1
651	Discontinued Operations					
652	Other-Related Companies	40.4	52.6	62.4	65.5	61.9
653	Other					
654	**TOTAL**	198.4	264.7	286.3	305.0	353.0
655	**% CHANGE IN NET OPERATING PROFIT BY DIVISION**					
656	Division 1-Heavy Building Materials		48.01%	24.45%	(1.00%)	
657	Division 2-Heating (Home Products to 1994)		4.19%	(74.52%)	104.68%	
658	Division 3-Bathrooms				(8.89%)	
659	Division 4-Property		115.69%	(70.00%)	260.61%	
660	Division 5-Other		(16.67%)	62.50%	(159.52%)	
661	Subtotal Continuing Operations		34.24%	5.56%	6.97%	21.54%
662	Discontinued Operations					
663	Other-Related Companies		30.20%	18.63%	4.97%	
664	Other					
665	**TOTAL**		33.42%	8.16%	6.53%	15.74%
666	**NET OPERATING PROFIT % OF SALES BY DIVISION**					
667	Division 1-Heavy Building Materials	11.87%	16.57%	19.46%	18.51%	
668	Division 2-Heating (Home Products to 1994)	7.84%	8.15%	2.61%	5.47%	
669	Division 3-Bathrooms			15.66%	14.04%	
670	Division 4-Property	21.16%	15.21%	19.41%	38.64%	
671	Division 5-Other	(147.69%)	(149.33%)	(300.00%)	(545.00%)	
672	Subtotal Continuing Operations	9.41%	11.92%	12.62%	13.20%	15.01%
673	Discontinued Operations					
674	Other-Related Companies	16.03%	18.63%	20.66%	19.00%	
675	Other					
676	**TOTAL**	10.28%	12.84%	13.79%	14.12%	15.22%

OPEN UNIVERSITY FINANCIAL SPREADSHEET

Company Name:	Blue Circle Industries PLC	Date: 12-Jun-98
Business:	Building Mat'ls & Property Dev't	Analyst: PAS
Currency:	Sterling Millions	
Domicile:	UK	

	BREAKDOWN BY AREA	31-Dec-93	31-Dec-94	31-Dec-95	31-Dec-96	31-Dec-97
710						
711	**SALES BY AREA**					
712	Area 1-Europe	1,198.1	1,281.2	1,208.8	1,196.1	1,140.0
713	Area 2-North America	324.1	359.6	396.5	439.9	635.6
714	Area 3-South America	109.4	115.6	145.2	170.6	171.2
715	Area 4-Africa	173.0	173.0	165.0	164.6	158.3
716	Area 5-Asia+Other	126.2	132.7	162.2	188.4	214.1
717	Subtotal Continuing Operations	1,930.8	2,062.1	2,077.7	2,159.6	2,319.2
718	Discontinued Operations					
719	Other					
720	Other					
721	**TOTAL**	1,930.8	2,062.1	2,077.7	2,159.6	2,319.2
722	**% CHANGE IN SALES**					
723	Area 1-Europe		6.94%	(5.65%)	(1.05%)	(4.69%)
724	Area 2-North America		10.95%	10.26%	10.95%	44.49%
725	Area 3-South America		5.67%	25.61%	17.49%	0.35%
726	Area 4-Africa			(4.62%)	(0.24%)	(3.83%)
727	Area 5-Asia+Other		5.15%	22.23%	16.15%	13.64%
728	Subtotal Continuing Operations		6.80%	0.76%	3.94%	7.39%
729	Discontinued Operations					
730	Other					
731	Other					
732	**TOTAL**		6.80%	0.76%	3.94%	7.39%
733	**SALES BY AREA AS % OF TOTAL SALES**					
734	Area 1-Europe	62.05%	62.13%	58.18%	55.39%	49.15%
735	Area 2-North America	16.79%	17.44%	19.08%	20.37%	27.41%
736	Area 3-South America	5.67%	5.61%	6.99%	7.90%	7.38%
737	Area 4-Africa	8.96%	8.39%	7.94%	7.62%	6.83%
738	Area 5-Asia+Other	6.54%	6.44%	7.81%	8.72%	9.23%
739	Subtotal Continuing Operations	100.00%	100.00%	100.00%	100.00%	100.00%
740	Discontinued Operations					
741	Other					
742	Other					
743	**TOTAL**	100.00%	100.00%	100.00%	100.00%	100.00%
744	**NET OPERATING PROFIT BY AREA**					
745	Area 1-Europe	92.6	128.7	109.3	123.4	151.7
746	Area 2-North America	32.6	48.6	63.5	75.3	114.3
747	Area 3-South America	34.5	35.4	45.5	43.1	34.0
748	Area 4-Africa	17.9	29.9	31.6	24.7	20.6
749	Area 5-Asia+Other	20.8	22.1	36.4	38.4	32.4
750	Subtotal Continuing Operations	198.4	264.7	286.3	304.9	353.0
751	Discontinued Operations					
752	Other					
753	Other					
754	**TOTAL**	198.4	264.7	286.3	304.9	353.0
755	**% CHANGE IN NET OPERATING PROFIT BY AREA**					
756	Area 1-Europe		38.98%	(15.07%)	12.90%	22.93%
757	Area 2-North America		49.08%	30.66%	18.58%	51.79%
758	Area 3-South America		2.61%	28.53%	(5.27%)	(21.11%)
759	Area 4-Africa		67.04%	5.69%	(21.84%)	(16.60%)
760	Area 5-Asia+Other		6.25%	64.71%	5.49%	(15.63%)
761	Subtotal Continuing Operations		33.42%	8.16%	6.50%	15.78%
762	Discontinued Operations					
763	Other					
764	Other					
765	**TOTAL**		33.42%	8.16%	6.50%	15.78%
766	**NET OPERATING PROFIT % OF SALES BY AREA**					
767	Area 1-Europe	7.73%	10.05%	9.04%	10.32%	13.31%
768	Area 2-North America	10.06%	13.52%	16.02%	17.12%	17.98%
769	Area 3-South America	31.54%	30.62%	31.34%	25.26%	19.86%
770	Area 4-Africa	10.35%	17.28%	19.15%	15.01%	13.01%
771	Area 5-Asia+Other	16.48%	16.65%	22.44%	20.38%	15.13%
772	Subtotal Continuing Operations	10.28%	12.84%	13.78%	14.12%	15.22%
773	Discontinued Operations					
774	Other					
775	Other					
776	**TOTAL**	10.28%	12.84%	13.78%	14.12%	15.22%

APPENDIX 3   BLUE CIRCLE INDUSTRIES PLC 1997 OUFS SPREADING NOTES

Line ref.	Spread caption	A/R page	Location of Information
	ASSETS		
111	Cash and Deposits	45	Cash at bank and in hand
112	Marketable Securities	45	Investments-deposits
114	Net Trade Receivables	57	Note 15; Trade Debtors (Adjusted for amounts falling due after 1 year)
119	Raw Materials	57	Note 14; Raw materials and stores
120	Work in Progress	57	Note 14; Work in progress
121	Finished Goods	57	Note 14; Finished goods
128	ACT Receivable	57	Note 15; Advance Corporation Tax (Adjusted for amounts falling due after 1 year)
133	Due From Related Companies	57	Note 15; Amounts owed by related companies
134	Other Receivables	57	Note 15; Other debtors (Adjusted for amounts falling due after 1 year)
136	Prepaid Expenses	57	Note 15; Prepayments (adjusted for amounts falling due after 1 year)
140	Land and Buildings – freehold	55	Note 12; Net Book Value, Freehold
141	Land and Buildings – long l'hold	55	Note 12; Net Book Value, Long lease
142	Land and Buildings – short l'hold	55	Note 12; Net Book Value, Short lease
143	Plant and Machinery	55	Note 12; Net Book Value, Plant and machinery
147	Construction in Progress	55	Note 12; Net Book Value, Assets under construction
150	Investments – Related Company	56	Note 13; Group- Related companies, Shares
151	Investments – Other	56	Note 13; Group- Other Investments *plus* Own Shares
152	Investments – Loans to Related Companies	56	Note 13; Group- Related company, Loans

157	Long Term Trade Receivables – Other Trade Receivables	57	Note 15; Included in the above are amounts falling due after one year: Trade debtors
162	Other Long Term Receivables – Other LT Receivables	57	Note 15; Included in the above are amounts falling due after one year: Other debtors
165	Long Term Tax Receivable – LT ACT Receivable	57	Note 15; Included in the above are amounts falling due after one year: Advance Corporation Tax
170	Prepaid Expenses	57	Note 15; Included in the above are amounts falling due after one year: Prepayments

LIABILITIES

212	Short Term Debt – Bank Loans	58	Note 17; Amounts falling due within one year: Bank loans and overdrafts – secured *plus* unsecured
215	Short Term Debt – Current Portion Long term Debt	58	Note 17; Amounts falling due within one year: Debentures and other loans – secured *plus* unsecured
216	Short Term Debt – Current Portion Lease Obligation	58	Note 17; Amounts falling due within one year: Leasing obligations
218	Trade Creditors	57	Note 16; Falling due within one year: Trade creditors
219	Accrued Expenses	57	Note 16; Falling due within one year: Accruals *plus* Other taxes and social security costs
222	Taxes Payable – Corporation Tax Payable	57	Note 16; Falling due within one year: Tax
225	Dividends Payable	57	Note 16; Falling due within one year: Proposed dividend
226	Due to Related Companies	57	Note 16; Falling due within one year: Amounts owed to related companies
227	Other Creditors	57	Note 16; Falling due within one year: Other creditors
237	Long Term Debt – Leases	58	Note 17; Leasing Obligations: Payable in more than one but less than five years
238	Long Term Debt – Bank Loans	58	Note 17; Amounts falling due after more than one year: Bank loans and overdrafts – secured *plus* unsecured

239	Long Term Debt – Bonds and Debentures	58	Note 17; Amounts falling due after more than one year: Debenture and other loans – secured *plus* unsecured
241	Long Term Debt – Convertible Long-Term Debt	58	Note 17; Amounts falling due after more than one year: Subordinated convertible bonds – unsecured
246	Long Term Taxes Payable – Corporation Taxes Payable	58	Note 16; Falling due after more than one year: Tax
249	Sundry Non Current Liabilities	45, 57	Note 16; Falling due after more than one year: Other taxes and social security costs *plus* Other creditors *plus* accruals *plus* Government Grants (*45*)
251	Deferred Taxation	60	Note 19; Deferred tax
254	Long Term Provisions – Restructuring	60	Note 19; Restructuring provisions
258	Minority Interests	45	Minority interests (all equity)
260	Ordinary Shares	45	Ordinary share capital
261	Preference Shares	45	Preference share capital
262	Share Premium	45	Share premium account
266	Revaluation Reserve	45	Revaluation reserve
268	Other Reserves – Unrestricted	45	Reserves of related companies
269	Profit and Loss Reserve	45	Profit and loss account
276	Contingent Liabilities	63	Note 23; Contingent liabilities
277	Acquisition of Subsidiary net of Cash	47	Group Cash Flow Statement: Acquisitions and disposals – Purchase of subsidiary
278	Book Value of Property, Plant and Equipment Sold	55	Note 12: Tangible Assets: Gross book value, Disposals *less* Depreciation, Disposals
279	Proceeds from the Sale of Property, Plant and Equipment	47	Group Cash Flow Statement: Capital expenditure and financial investment, Disposal of tangible fixed assets
280	Property, Plant and Equipment Revaluation for the year	55	Note 12; Group – Gross book value, Revaluation

281	Foreign Exchange relating to plant	55	Note 12; Group – Gross book value, Exchange rate and other adjustments minus Depreciation, Exchange rate and other adjustments
282	Number of Shares Issued and Outstanding	68	Group Five Year Statement – Issued ordinary shares
283	Date of Share Price	68	Group Five Year Statement – Share price during year
284	Share Price	68	Group Five Year Statement – Share price during year – high
285	Earnings per Share	68	Earnings per share
286	Dividends per Share	68	Dividends per share
287	No. of Days in Accounting Period	44	Group Profit and Loss Account – Year ended 1997 *less* year ended 1996

INCOME STATEMENT

312	Total Sales	44	Turnover - Total *less* Turnover of related companies
313	Cost of Goods Sold	44	Cost of Sales
314	Selling and Distribution Expenses	52	Note 3; Net operating expenses – Distribution costs
315	Administrative Expenses	52	Note 3; Net operating expenses – Administration expenses
316	Other Operating Income	52	Note 3; Other operating income
318	Exceptional Items	44	Loss on disposal of discontinued businesses
320	For Information – Depreciation	52	Note 5; Depreciation
324	For Information – Operating Leases, Plant and Equipment	52	Note 5; Operating lease rentals: Plant and machinery
325	For Information – Operating Leases, Other	52	Note 5; Operating lease rentals: Other
328	Research and Development	52	Note 5; Research and development expenditure
329	Wages and Salaries	53	Note 6; Wages and salaries
337	Interest Expense	53	Note 7; Total of interest payable
340	Interest Income	53	Note 7; Interest receivable
343	Equity Income – Associates	44 , 48	Share of Profits of Related Company *minus* Notes to the Group Cash Flow Statement: Dividends received from related company.

344	Dividend Income	48	Notes to the Group Cash Flow Statement; Dividends received from related company
353	Corporation Tax-Domestic	53	Note 8; Corporation tax at 31.5%
354	Corporation Tax-Overseas	53	Note 8; Overseas tax
355	Deferred Tax	53	Note 8; Deferred tax
356	Prior Year Adjustment	53	Note 8; Adjustment for prior years
357	Other Tax	53	Note 8; (Double tax relief) *plus* ACT written off *plus* Tax on share of profit of related companies
361	Minority Interest-share of RE	45	Minority Interests
363	Dividends – Ordinary	44	Dividends: Ordinary
364	Dividends – Preference	44	Dividends: Preference
369	Adjustment to Profit and Loss Reserve: Goodwill Written Back	62	Note 21: Goodwill
370	Adjustment to Profit and Loss Reserve: Foreign Exchange Translation	62	Note 21; Profit and loss account: Exchange gains (losses) on retranslation *plus* Exchange gains (losses) on foreign currency borrowings.
371	Adjustment to Profit and Loss Reserve: Transfer to/from reserves	62	Note 21; Profit and loss account: Transfer and changes in Group interests *plus* Movements relating to QUEST *minus* Reserves of related companies: Retained profit for the year. (*As it has already been included in the profit and loss for the financial year – line 336*)
375	Other Adjustments to Shareholders' Equity: Shares Issued	61	Note 20; Ordinary Shares of 50p: Issued 1997 *minus* Issued 1996.
376	Other Adjustments to Shareholders' Equity: Share Issue Premium	62	Note 21; Premium on issues less expenses *plus* Transfers and changes in Group interests
379	Preference Shares Issued	61	Note 20; Preference Shares 1997 *minus* 1996 (conversions)
383	Other Adjustments to Shareholders' Equity: Foreign Exchange Translation	62	Note 21; Reserves of related companies: Exchange gain/(losses) on retranslation *plus* Exchange gains/(losses) on foreign currency borrowings

| 384 | Other Adjustments to Shareholders' Equity: Revaluation for the year | 62 | Note 21; Revaluation reserves: Surplus arising on revaluation *plus* Exchange losses on retranslation *plus* Transfer and changes in Group interests |
| 385 | Transfer to/from Reserves | 62 | Note 21; Other reserves: Transfer and changes in Group interests *plus* Reserves of related companies: Retained profit for the year. |

DIVISIONAL INFORMATION

612	Sales by Division: Division 1 – Heavy Building Materials	50	Note 2; Segmental analysis, Class of business *less* Related companies (group share)
613	Sales by Division: Division 2 – Heating	50	Note 2; Segmental analysis, Class of business
614	Sales by Division: Division 3 – Bathrooms	50	Note 2; Segmental analysis, Class of business
615	Sales by Division: Division 4 – Property	50	Note 2; Segmental analysis, Class of business *less* Related companies (group share)
616	Sales by Division: Division 5 – Other	50	Note 2; Segmental analysis, Class of business
619	Sales by Division: Other – Related Companies	50	Note 2; Segmental analysis, Class of business
645	Net Operating Profit by Division: Division 1 – Heavy Building Materials	50	Note 2; Segmental analysis, Class of business *less* Related companies (group share)
646	Net Operating Profit by Division: Division 2 – Heating	50	Note 2; Segmental analysis, Class of business
647	Net Operating Profit by Division: Division 3 – Bathrooms	50	Note 2; Segmental analysis, Class of business
648	Net Operating Profit by Division: Division 4 – Property	50	Note 2; Segmental analysis, Class of business *less* Related companies (group share)
649	Net Operating Profit by Division: Division 5 – Other	50	Note 2; Segmental analysis, Class of business
652	Net Operating Profit by Division: Other – Related Companies	50	Note 2; Segmental analysis, Class of business

GEOGRAPHICAL INFORMATION

| 712 | Sales by Area: Area 1 – Europe | 50 | Note 2; Segmental analysis, Geographical Analysis |
| 713 | Sales by Area: Area 2 – North America | 50 | Note 2; Segmental analysis, Geographical Analysis |

714	Sales by Area: Area 3 – South America	50	Note 2; Segmental analysis, Geographical Analysis
715	Sales by Area: Area 4 – Africa	50	Note 2; Segmental analysis, Geographical Analysis
716	Sales by Area: Area 5 – Asia + Other Areas	50	Note 2; Segmental analysis, Geographical Analysis
745	Net Operating Profit by Area: Area 1 – Europe	51	Note 2; Segmental analysis, Geographical Analysis
746	Net Operating Profit by Area: Area 2 – North America	51	Note 2; Segmental analysis, Geographical Analysis
747	Net Operating Profit by Area: Area 3 – South America	51	Note 2; Segmental analysis, Geographical Analysis
748	Net Operating Profit by Area: Area 4 – Africa	51	Note 2; Segmental analysis, Geographical Analysis
749	Net Operating Profit by Area: Area 5 – Asia + Other Areas	51	Note 2; Segmental analysis, Geographical Analysis

APPENDIX 4   PORTER CHECKLIST

Threat of new entrants

The following factors act to *discourage* new entrants to an industry:

- Economies of scale (for example: production, research, marketing, service, distribution, sales force, financing)
- Product differentiation (for example: brand identification)
- Capital requirements (for example: fixed assets, customer credit, inventories, start-up losses)
- Cost disadvantages independent of size (for example: learning/ experience curve, proprietary technology, access to raw materials assets purchased at pre-inflationary prices, government subsidies, favourable locations)
- Access to distribution channels; or
- Government policy (for example: licensing, safety and environmental regulations).

Bargaining power of customers

The following factors will *limit* the profits that can be achieved in an industry:

- Few or large volume buyers
- Standard or undifferentiated products
- Product represents a significant proportion of the buyer's costs
- Buyer is in a low profit industry
- Product is unimportant to the quality of the buyer's product or service
- Product does not save the buyer money; or
- Buyer poses a threat of backward integration.

Bargaining power of suppliers

The following factors will also *limit* the profit that can be achieved in an industry:

- Supplier's industry is dominated by a few companies or is more concentrated than the industry it is selling to
- Input is unique, differentiated or has switching costs
- Input can not be easily substituted by a similar product
- Supplier poses a threat of forward integration; or
- Industry is not an important customer of the supplier.

Threat of substitute products or services

The availability of alternate products which could be substituted for the industry's output will limit the price and hence the profit that can be achieved in that industry.

Jockeying among current contestants

Intense rivalry, limiting the total profit achieved by all players in an industry, will increase with the following factors:

- Numerous players of roughly equal size
- A slow rate of growth in the industry
- Lack of differentiation or switching costs
- Fixed costs represent a high proportion of total costs
- Capacity that can be increased only in large increments
- High exit barriers; or
- Rivals diverse in strategy, origin and 'personality'.

APPENDIX 5 ALBERT FISHER OUFS

OPEN UNIVERSITY FINANCIAL SPREADSHEET

Company Name:	Albert Fisher Group PLC	Date: 01-Jul-98
Business:	Food Processing and Distribution	Analyst: PAS
Currency:	Sterling Millions	
Domicile:	UK	

	SUMMARY		30-Aug-92	30-Aug-93	30-Aug-94	30-Aug-95	30-Aug-96
809	**SUMMARY**						
810							
811	**A S S E T S**	Line Reference					
812	Cash. Deposits and Marketable Securities	111+112	215.7	53.2	64.5	66.8	51.4
813	Trade Receivables	117	104.8	120.6	140.9	143.9	139.3
814	Inventory	125	102.3	108.0	130.4	135.7	149.1
815	Other Current Assets	131+135+136+137	23.6	29.5	31.6	30.9	26.5
816	**Current Assets**	138	**446.4**	**311.3**	**367.4**	**377.3**	**366.3**
817	Net Property, Plant and Equipment	148	159.3	191.2	222.8	223.4	240.0
818	Investments	153	12.4	10.0	11.4	14.4	12.0
819	Long Term Receivables	158+163	2.9	3.2	0.7	0.3	0.6
820	Other Long Term Assets	169+170:172	3.8	3.3	3.4	3.4	3.4
821	Intangibles	178	0.0	0.0	0.0	0.0	0.0
822	**Non Current Assets**	179	**178.4**	**207.7**	**238.3**	**241.5**	**256.0**
823	**TOTAL ASSETS**	181	**624.8**	**519.0**	**605.7**	**618.8**	**622.3**
824							
825	**LIABILITIES**						
826	Short Term Debt	217	11.3	46.3	77.7	31.1	33.5
827	Trade Creditors	218	100.2	123.4	165.2	172.5	156.8
828	Accrued Expenses	219	17.8	24.7	25.4	30.2	31.8
829	Other Current Liabilities	220+224:7+233+234	41.1	56.2	56.4	72.1	88.2
830	**Current Liabilities**	235	**170.4**	**250.6**	**324.7**	**305.9**	**310.3**
831	Long Term Debt	244	174.8	82.8	80.2	133.9	157.2
832	Other Non Current Liabilities	248+249	8.8	4.0	2.0	1.0	1.7
833	**Total Liabilities**	250	**354.0**	**337.4**	**406.9**	**440.8**	**469.2**
834	Deferred Taxation	251	1.6	1.5	3.1	1.1	1.5
835	Long Term Provisions:	257	0.0	0.0	0.0	0.0	0.0
836	Minority Interests	258	3.0	0.8	1.2	2.4	2.8
837	**Total Liabilities and Provisions**	259	**358.6**	**339.7**	**411.2**	**444.3**	**473.5**
838	Share Capital	260:263	156.4	71.9	124.4	94.3	94.4
839	Other Reserves	264:268	24.4	29.7	(4.4)	6.5	27.5
840	Profit and Loss Reserve	269	85.4	77.7	74.5	73.7	26.9
841	**Shareholder's Equity**	270	**266.2**	**179.3**	**194.5**	**174.5**	**148.8**
842	**TOTAL LIABILITIES & EQUITY**	272	**624.8**	**519.0**	**605.7**	**618.8**	**622.3**
843							
844	**INCOME STATEMENT**						
845	**TOTAL SALES**	312	**1,197.6**	**1,284.2**	**1,424.4**	**1,649.9**	**1,697.9**
846	Cost of Goods Sold	313	(989.6)	(1,053.4)	(1,208.3)	(1,419.1)	(1,463.8)
847	Selling & Distribution Expenses	314	(117.0)	(132.4)	(116.2)	(120.7)	(118.7)
848	Administrative Expense	315	(45.6)	(54.0)	(62.0)	(70.6)	(67.5)
849	Other Operating Income/Expenses	316:317	6.8	3.5	3.0	(1.3)	(0.3)
850	Exceptional Items	318	0.0	0.0	0.0	0.0	0.0
851	**NET OPERATING PROFIT (NOP)**	336	**52.2**	**47.9**	**40.9**	**38.2**	**47.6**
852	Net Interest Expense	337:340	(20.0)	(20.2)	(11.3)	(13.7)	(18.4)
853	Other Financial Income/Expense	341:344	26.5	17.4	5.2	6.6	10.9
854	**PROFIT AFTER FINANCIAL ITEMS**	345	**58.7**	**45.1**	**34.8**	**31.1**	**40.1**
855	Other Income/Expense	346:349	0.0	0.0	0.0	0.0	0.0
856	Exceptional Income/Expense	350+351	(34.2)	(15.4)	0.0	0.0	(151.0)
857	**PRE TAX PROFIT**	352	**24.5**	**29.7**	**34.8**	**31.1**	**(110.9)**
858	Taxes	353:357	(14.3)	(11.2)	(12.9)	(10.3)	(10.4)
859	**NET PROFIT AFTER TAX (NPAT)**	358	**10.2**	**18.5**	**21.9**	**20.8**	**(121.3)**
860	Extraordinary Income/Expense	359+360	0.0	0.0	0.0	0.0	0.0
861	Minority Interest	361	0.2	0.0	(0.4)	(0.2)	(0.4)
862	Dividends	362:365	(24.6)	(24.8)	(24.7)	(26.7)	(26.8)
863	**RETAINED PROFIT OR LOSS FOR THE YEAR**	366	**(14.2)**	**(6.3)**	**(3.2)**	**(6.1)**	**(148.5)**
864							
865	**RATIO SUMMARY**						
866	Return on Equity (NPAT/Equity %)	416	3.83	10.32	11.26	11.92	(81.52)
867	Return on Sales (NPAT/Sales %)	413	0.85	1.44	1.54	1.26	(7.14)
868	Asset Turnover (Sales/Total Assets)	414	1.92	2.47	2.35	2.67	2.73
869	Asset Leverage (Total Assets/Equity)	415	2.35	2.89	3.11	3.55	4.18
870	Net Operating Assets/Sales (%)	427	8.13	7.53	6.94	5.59	6.67
871	Current Ratio	433	2.62	1.24	1.13	1.23	1.18
872	Gross Gearing (%)	436	69.91	72.00	81.18	94.56	128.16
873	Leverage (Gross)	438	1.33	1.88	2.09	2.53	3.15
874	Net Operating Profit / Sales (%)	453	4.36	3.73	2.87	2.32	2.80
875	Net Operating Profit/Interest Expense	454	2.6	2.4	3.6	2.8	2.6
876	NOP - Taxes Paid (= NOPAT)(Sterling Millions)	462	na	34.5	28.9	34.3	40.9
877	NOPAT/Interest Paid + CPLTD & L+ Divs. Paid	465	na	0.77	0.41	0.30	0.55
878	Operating Free Cash Flow (OFCF)	553	na	54.8	25.9	46.6	34.2
879	OFCF/Int. Paid + CPLTD &L+Divs. Paid	468	na	1.22	0.37	0.41	0.46
880	Market Capitalisation (Millions)	486	0.0	0.0	0.0	0.0	0.0

OPEN UNIVERSITY FINANCIAL SPREADSHEET

Company Name:	Albert Fisher Group PLC				Date: 01-Jul-98
Business:	Food Processing and Distribution				Analyst: PAS
Currency:	Sterling	Units: Millions			
Domicile:	UK				Auditor: Ernst & Young

	ASSETS	30-Aug-92	30-Aug-93	30-Aug-94	30-Aug-95	30-Aug-96
111	Cash and Deposits	215.7	53.1	64.4	66.7	51.3
112	Marketable Securities	0.0	0.1	0.1	0.1	0.1
113	Trade Receivables:					
114	-Net Trade Receivables	104.8	120.6	140.9	143.9	139.3
115	- Recoverable under Contracts					
116	-Other Trade Receivables					
117	*Sub Total Trade Receivables*	104.8	120.6	140.9	143.9	139.3
118	Inventory:					
119	- Raw Materials	34.8	18.3	32.4	43.4	47.6
120	- Work in Progress	0.5	2.7	6.6	7.8	7.4
121	- Finished Goods	67.0	87.0	91.4	84.5	94.1
122	- Advance Payments to Suppliers					
123	- Progress Payments					
124	- Development Properties					
125	*Sub Total Inventory*	102.3	108.0	130.4	135.7	149.1
127	Tax Receivable:					
128	-ACT Receivable					
129	-Corporation Tax Receivable					
130	-Other Tax Receivable					
131	*Sub Total Tax Receivable*	0.0	0.0	0.0	0.0	0.0
132	Other Receivables					
133	-Due from Related Companies					
134	-Other Receivables	15.3	13.3	13.4	15.6	13.1
135	*Sub Total Other Receivables*	15.3	13.3	13.4	15.6	13.1
136	Prepaid Expenses	8.3	16.2	18.2	15.3	13.4
137	Sundry Current Assets					
138	**CURRENT ASSETS**	446.4	311.3	367.4	377.3	366.3
139	Net Property, Plant and Equipment:					
140	-Land and Buildings - Freehold	89.2	107.5	119.0	121.7	130.5
141	-Long Leasehold	5.9	6.9	5.7	5.8	5.7
142	-Short Leasehold	4.1	7.9	11.9	12.1	12.8
143	-Plant and Machinery	60.1	68.9	86.2	83.8	91.0
144	-Fixtures and Fittings					
145	-Other Fixed Assets (Depreciable)					
146	-Other Fixed Assets (Non Depreciable)					
147	-Construction in Progress					
148	*Sub Total Net Property, Plant and Equipment*	159.3	191.2	222.8	223.4	240.0
149	Investments:					
150	-Related Company	12.4	10.0	11.3	13.0	11.0
151	-Other			0.1	1.4	1.0
152	-Loans to Related Companies					
153	*Sub Total Investments*	12.4	10.0	11.4	14.4	12.0
154	Long Term Trade Receivables:					
155	- Related Companies					
156	-Trade Loans					
157	-Other Trade Receivables					
158	*Sub Total LT Trade Receivables*	0.0	0.0	0.0	0.0	0.0
159	Other Long Term Receivables:					
160	- Related Companies					
161	-Non Trade Loans					
162	-Other LT Receivables	2.9	3.2	0.7	0.3	0.6
163	*Sub Total Other LT Receivables*	2.9	3.2	0.7	0.3	0.6
164	Long Term Tax Receivable:					
165	-LT ACT Receivable	3.8	3.3	3.4	3.4	3.4
166	-LT Corporation Tax Receivable					
167	-Deferred Tax					
168	-Other LT Tax Receivable					
169	*Sub Total Long Term Tax Receivable*	3.8	3.3	3.4	3.4	3.4
170	Prepaid Expenses					
171	Assets held for Sale (ST & LT)					
172	Sundry Non Current Assets					
173	Intangibles :					
174	Goodwill					
175	-Other Amortising					
176	-Other Nonamortising					
177	- Other					
178	*Sub Total Intangibles*	0.0	0.0	0.0	0.0	0.0
179	**NON CURRENT ASSETS**	178.4	207.7	238.3	241.5	256.0
181	**TOTAL ASSETS**	624.8	519.0	605.7	618.8	622.3

NOTES TO THE BALANCE SHEET:

OPEN UNIVERSITY FINANCIAL SPREADSHEET

Company Name:	Albert Fisher Group PLC	Date: 01-Jul-98
Business:	Food Processing and Distribution	Analyst: PAS
Currency:	Sterling Millions	
Domicile	UK	

	LIABILITIES	30-Aug-92	30-Aug-93	30-Aug-94	30-Aug-95	30-Aug-96
210						
211	Short Term Debt:					
212	- Bank Loans	11.3	9.8	3.6	2.5	8.4
213	- Other					
214	-Bills of Exchange Payable					
215	-Current Portion Long Term Debt		36.5	74.1	28.6	25.1
216	-Current Portion Lease Obligations					
217	**Sub Total Short Term Debt**	11.3	46.3	77.7	31.1	33.5
218	Trade Creditors	100.2	123.4	165.2	172.5	156.8
219	Accrued Expenses	17.8	24.7	25.4	30.2	31.8
220	Customer Prepayments					
221	Taxes Payable:					
222	-Corporation Tax Payable	10.2	7.7	7.0	14.8	19.1
223	-Other Taxes Payable					
224	**Sub Total Taxes Payable**	10.2	7.7	7.0	14.8	19.1
225	Dividends Payable	11.9	11.9	13.5	13.6	13.6
226	Due to Related Companies					
227	Other Creditors	19.0	36.6	35.9	43.7	55.5
228	Current Provisions:					
229	-Acquisition					
230	-Restructuring					
231	-Retirement /Employee Benefits					
232	-Other Provisions					
233	**Sub Total Current Provisions**	0.0	0.0	0.0	0.0	0.0
234	Other Current Liabilities					
235	**CURRENT LIABILITIES**	170.4	250.6	324.7	305.9	310.3
236	Long Term Debt:					
237	-Leases					
238	-Bank Loans	174.8	82.8	28.1	29.3	53.6
239	-Bonds and Debentures			52.1	104.6	103.6
240	-Other Long Term Debt					
241	-Convertible Long Term Debt					
242	-Subordinated Debt					
243	-Redeemable Preference Shares					
244	**Sub Total Long Term Debt**	174.8	82.8	80.2	133.9	157.2
245	Long Term Taxes Payable:					
246	-Corporation Tax Payable	0.4	0.3	0.4	1.0	0.0
247	-Other Taxes Payable					
248	**Sub Total Long TermTaxes Payable**	0.4	0.3	0.4	1.0	0.0
249	Sundry Non Current Liabilities	8.4	3.7	1.6	0.0	1.7
250	**TOTAL LIABILITIES**	354.0	337.4	406.9	440.8	469.2
251	Deferred Taxation	1.6	1.5	3.1	1.1	1.5
252	Long Term Provisions:					
253	-Acquisition					
254	-Restructuring					
255	-Retirement /Employee Benefits					
256	-Other Provisions					
257	**Sub Total Long Term Provisions**	0.0	0.0	0.0	0.0	0.0
258	Minority Interests	3.0	0.8	1.2	2.4	2.8
259	**TOTAL LIABILITIES AND PROVISIONS**	358.6	339.7	411.2	444.3	473.5
260	Ordinary Shares	30.0	30.0	35.4	35.6	35.8
261	Preference Shares	36.5				
262	Share Premium	89.9	41.9	89.0	58.7	58.6
263	Other Share Related					
264	Consolidation Differences					
265	Foreign Exchange Reserve					
266	Revaluation Reserve	6.9	6.9	6.9	3.4	3.4
267	Other Reserves - Restricted	17.5	22.8	(11.3)	3.1	24.1
268	Other Reserves -Unrestricted					
269	Profit and Loss Reserve	85.4	77.7	74.5	73.7	26.9
270	**SHAREHOLDERS' EQUITY**	266.2	179.3	194.5	174.5	148.8
271						
272	**TOTAL LIABILITIES & EQUITY**	624.8	519.0	605.7	618.8	622.3
273	Cross Check	0.0	0.0	0.0	0.0	0.0
275	**ADDITIONAL BALANCE SHEET INFORMATION:**					
276	Contingent Liabilities	0.0	0.0	0.0	31.8	0.0
277	Acquisition of Subsidiary net of Cash					
278	Book Value Property, Plant and Equipment Sold (Input Negative)	(10.9)	(7.4)	(9.0)	(19.7)	(8.7)
279	Proceeds from Sale of Property, Plant and Equipment	0.9	5.6	4.1	1.1	0.5
280	Property, Plant and Equipment Revaluation for the year					
281	Foreign Exchange relating to plant	(4.7)	19.2	0.9	5.0	(1.8)
282	Number of Shares Issued & Outstanding (In Thousands)	613,300.0	617,900.0	707,600.0	711,900.0	715,200.0
283	Date of Share Price					
284	Share Price					
285	Earnings per Share	0.017	0.024	0.033	0.029	(0.171)
286	Dividends per Share	0.037	0.037	0.037	0.038	0.038
287	No. of Days in Accounting Period	365	365	365	365	365

OPEN UNIVERSITY FINANCIAL SPREADSHEET

Company Name:	Albert Fisher Group PLC	Date: 01-Jul-98
Business:	Food Processing and Distribution	Analyst: PAS
Currency:	Sterling Millions	
Domicile	UK	

	INCOME STATEMENT	30-Aug-92	30-Aug-93	30-Aug-94	30-Aug-95	30-Aug-96
310						
311						
312	**TOTAL SALES**	**1,197.6**	**1,284.2**	**1,424.4**	**1,649.9**	**1,697.9**
313	Cost of Goods Sold	(989.6)	(1,053.4)	(1,208.3)	(1,419.1)	(1,463.8)
314	Selling & Distribution Expenses	(117.0)	(132.4)	(116.2)	(120.7)	(118.7)
315	Administrative Expense	(45.6)	(54.0)	(62.0)	(70.6)	(67.5)
316	Other Operating Income	6.8	3.5	2.4	7.1	1.8
317	Other Operating Expenses			0.6	(8.4)	(2.1)
318	Exceptional Items					
319	*For Information - Included in Operating Profit:*					
320	*Depreciation Manufacturer*	*(14.3)*	*(15.5)*	*(16.6)*	*(18.2)*	*(19.4)*
321	* Trader*					
322	*Amortisation*					
323	*Operating Leases Property*					
324	* Plant & Equipment*	*(9.4)*	*(7.0)*	*(7.0)*	*(13.3)*	*(13.9)*
325	* Other*					
326	*Personnel*					
327	*Advertising*					
328	*Research & Development*					
329	*Wages & salaries*					
330	*Material Expenses*					
331	*Gain/(Loss) Sale of Fixed Asset*	*(10.0)*	*(1.8)*	*(4.9)*	*(18.6)*	*(8.2)*
332	*Gain/(Loss) Sale of Associate*					
333	*Gain/(Loss) Sale of Investment*					
334	*Royalty Income*					
335	*Foreign Exchange*					
336	**NET OPERATING PROFIT (NOP)**	**52.2**	**47.9**	**40.9**	**38.2**	**47.6**
337	Interest Expense	(20.0)	(20.2)	(11.3)	(13.7)	(18.4)
338	Interest Provisions (Non Cash)					
339	(Capitalised Interest)					
340	Interest Income					
341	Other Financial Income	25.3	15.4	3.2	4.6	8.4
342	Other Financial Expense					
343	Equity Income - Associates	1.2	2.0	2.0	2.0	2.5
344	Dividend Income					
345	**PROFIT AFTER FINANCIAL ITEMS**	**58.7**	**45.1**	**34.8**	**31.1**	**40.1**
346	Sundry Income					
347	Sundry Expense					
348	Gain / Loss on Sale of Fixed Assets					
349	Gain / Loss on Sale of Investment					
350	Exceptional Income					
351	Exceptional Expense	(34.2)	(15.4)			(151.0)
352	**PRE TAX PROFIT**	**24.5**	**29.7**	**34.8**	**31.1**	**(110.9)**
353	Corporation Tax - Domestic	(9.6)	(8.5)	(8.4)	(7.7)	(5.9)
354	Corporation Tax - Overseas	(4.4)	(3.8)	(5.2)	(3.8)	(3.6)
355	Deferred Tax	0.1	0.6	0.1	1.5	(0.5)
356	Prior Year Adjustment	(0.4)	0.5	1.0	0.0	1.9
357	Other Tax			(0.4)	(0.3)	(2.3)
358	**NET PROFIT AFTER TAX (NPAT)**	**10.2**	**18.5**	**21.9**	**20.8**	**(121.3)**
359	Extraordinary Income					
360	Extraordinary Expense					
361	Minority Interest - Share of RE	0.2		(0.4)	(0.2)	(0.4)
362	Minority Interest - Dividends Paid					
363	Dividends - Ordinary	(22.5)	(22.7)	(24.7)	(26.7)	(26.8)
364	Dividends - Preference	(2.1)	(2.1)			
365	Dividends - Scrip					
366	**RETAINED PROFIT OR LOSS FOR THE FINANCIAL YEAR**	**(14.2)**	**(6.3)**	**(3.2)**	**(6.1)**	**(148.5)**
367	*Adjustments to* Prior Year					
368	*Profit & Loss* Goodwill Written Off					
369	*Reserve:* Goodwill Written Back					
370	Foreign Exchange Translation					
371	Transfer to/from Reserves				1.8	100.0
372	Other	(2.6)	(1.4)		3.5	1.7
373	**CHANGE IN PROFIT AND LOSS RESERVE**	**(16.8)**	**(7.7)**	**(3.2)**	**(0.8)**	**(46.8)**
374	*Other Adjustments* Prior Year					
375	*to Shareholders'* Shares Issued		0.2	5.2	0.2	
376	*Equity:* Share Issue Premium			47.1	(30.3)	(0.1)
377	Shares Issued for Scrip Dividends					
378	Shares Repurchased		(36.5)			
379	Preference Shares Issued					
380	Other Share related	0.3				
381	Goodwill Written Off	(35.9)	(47.7)	(43.1)	(20.2)	(7.0)
382	Goodwill Written Back	12.7	8.0	8.0	3.8	128.9
383	Foreign Exchange Translation	1.7	(5.0)	1.0	0.8	0.9
384	Revaluation for the Year				(3.5)	
385	Transfer to/from Reserves					(100.0)
386	Other	0.3	1.8	0.2	30.0	(1.6)
387	**CHANGE IN SHAREHOLDER'S EQUITY**	**(37.7)**	**(86.9)**	**15.2**	**(20.0)**	**(25.7)**
388	Cross Check Profit & Loss	na	0.0	0.0	0.0	0.0
389	Shareholders Equity	na	0.0	0.0	0.0	0.0

OPEN UNIVERSITY FINANCIAL SPREADSHEET

Company Name:	Albert Fisher Group PLC		Date: 01-Jul-98
Business:	Food Processing and Distribution		Analyst: PAS
Currency:	Sterling Millions		
Domicile:	UK		

	RATIO ANALYSIS	Line Reference	30-Aug-92	30-Aug-93	30-Aug-94	30-Aug-95	30-Aug-96
410							
411							
412	**CORE RATIOS**						
413	Return on Sales (NPAT/Sales %)	358/312	0.85	1.44	1.54	1.26	(7.14)
414	Asset Turnover (Sales/Total Assets)	312/181	1.92	2.47	2.35	2.67	2.73
415	Asset Leverage (Total Assets/Equity)	181/270	2.35	2.89	3.11	3.55	4.18
416	Return on Equity (NPAT/Equity %)	358/270	3.83	10.32	11.26	11.92	(81.52)
417							
418	**OPERATING EFFICIENCY**						
419	Trade Creditor Days	218*287/313	36.96	42.76	49.90	44.37	39.10
420	Accrued Expenses Days	219*287/313	6.57	8.56	7.67	7.77	7.93
421	Inventory Days	125*287/313	37.73	37.42	39.39	34.90	37.18
422	- Raw Materials Days	119*287/313	12.84	6.34	9.79	11.16	11.87
423	- Work in Progress Days	120*287/313	0.18	0.94	1.99	2.01	1.85
424	- Finished Goods Days	121*287/313	24.71	30.15	27.61	21.73	23.46
425	Trade Receivables Days	117*287/313	31.94	34.28	36.11	31.83	29.95
426	Net Operating Assets (Sterling Millions)	117+125+136-218-219	97	97	99	92	113
427	Net Operating Assets/Sales (%)	426/312	8.13	7.53	6.94	5.59	6.67
428	Net Property Plant & Equipment T/O(Sales/NetPP&E)	312/148	7.52	6.72	6.39	7.39	7.07
429	Cash & Marketable Securities/Sales (%)	111+112/312	18.01	4.14	4.53	4.05	3.03
430	Cash & Marketable Securities/Current Assets (%)	111+112/138	48.32	17.09	17.56	17.70	14.03
431							
432	**FINANCIAL STRUCTURE**						
433	Current Ratio	138/235	2.62	1.24	1.13	1.23	1.18
434	Quick Ratio	138-125/235	2.02	0.81	0.73	0.79	0.70
435	Working Capital (Sterling Millions)	138-235	276	61	43	71	56
436	Gross Gearing (%)	217+244/270	69.91	72.00	81.18	94.56	128.16
437	Net Gearing (%)	217+244-111-112/270	(11.12)	42.33	48.02	56.28	93.62
438	Leverage (Gross)	250/270	1.33	1.88	2.09	2.53	3.15
439	Leverage (Tangible Inc. Contingents)	250+276/270-178	1.33	1.88	2.09	2.71	3.15
440	Leverage (Tangible)	250/270-178	1.33	1.88	2.09	2.53	3.15
441	Total Liabilities / Market Cap	250/486	0.00	0.00	0.00	0.00	0.00
442	Total Debt(ST +LT)/Total Debt + Equity	217+244/217+244+270	0.41	0.42	0.45	0.49	0.56
443	Capital Employed(Sterling Millions)	217+244+248.9+257.8+270	464	313	356	343	344
444	Total Liabilities/Capital Employed	250/443	0.76	1.08	1.14	1.29	1.36
445	Average Debt (Sterling Millions)	(217+244)/2	na	157.6	143.5	161.5	177.9
446	Int.Expense/Average Debt (%)	337/445	na	12.82	7.87	8.49	10.35
447							
448	**PROFITABILITY**						
449	Sales (Sterling Millions)	312	1,198	1,284	1,424	1,650	1,698
450	Change in Sales (%)	312	na	7.23	10.92	15.83	2.91
451	Cost of Goods Sold / Sales (%)	313/312	82.63	82.03	84.83	86.01	86.21
452	Selling & Distribution Expense s / Sales (%)	314/312	9.77	10.31	8.16	7.32	6.99
453	Net Operating Profit / Sales (%)	336/312	4.36	3.73	2.87	2.32	2.80
454	Net Operating Profit/Interest Expense	336/337	2.61	2.37	3.62	2.79	2.59
455	Pre-Tax Profit / Sales (%)	352/312	2.05	2.31	2.44	1.88	(6.53)
456	Effective Tax Rate (%)	353..357/352	58.37	37.71	37.07	33.12	(9.38)
457	Net Profit after Tax / Sales (%)	358/312	0.85	1.44	1.54	1.26	(7.14)
458	Dividends/Net Profit after Tax (%)	362..365/358	241.18	134.05	112.79	128.37	(22.09)
459							
460	**CASHFLOW RATIOS**						
461	EBITDA / Sales (%)	514/312	na	4.9	4.0	3.4	3.9
462	NOP - Taxes Paid (= NOPAT)(Sterling Millions)	512 - 524	na	35	29	34	41
463	NOPAT/Interest Paid	462/525	na	1.71	2.56	2.50	2.22
464	NOPAT/Interest Paid + CPLTD & L	462/(525+526)	na	1.71	0.60	0.39	0.87
465	NOPAT/Interest Paid + CPLTD & L+ Divs. Paid	462/(525+526+528)	na	0.77	0.41	0.30	0.55
466	Operating Free Cash Flow(OFCF)/Interest Paid	553/525	na	2.71	2.29	3.40	1.86
467	OFCF/Int. Paid + CPLTD &L	553/(525+526)	na	2.71	0.54	0.53	0.73
468	OFCF/Int. Paid + CPLTD &L+Divs. Paid	553/(525+526+528)	na	1.22	0.37	0.41	0.46
469	Net Expenditure Property, Plant & Equipment (Millions)	532	na	(30)	(52)	(32)	(46)
470	Net Expenditure PP&E/Total Assets (%)	469/181	na	5.78	8.62	5.24	7.39
471	Net Expenditure PP&E/Sales %	469/312	na	2.34	3.66	1.96	2.71
472	Depn./Net Expenditure PP&E	(320+321)/469	na	0.52	0.32	0.56	0.42
473	Depreciation/Net PP&E (%)	(320+321)/148	8.98	8.11	7.45	8.15	8.08
474	Years to Repay Debt (Debt/NOPAT-Int. Paid)	(217+244)/(462-525)	na	9.03	8.97	8.01	8.48
475							
476							
477	**MARKET RELATED DATA**						
478	Number of Shares Issued & Outstanding(In Thousands)	282	613,300	617,900	707,600	711,900	715,200
479	Date of Share Price	283	0	0	0	0	0
480	Share Price	284	0.00	0.00	0.00	0.00	0.00
481	Earnings per Share	285	0.017	0.024	0.033	0.029	(0.171)
482	Dividend per Share	286	0.037	0.037	0.037	0.038	0.038
483	Change in Dividend per Share (%)	482	na	0.00	0.00	2.70	0.00
484	Number of Days in Period Days	287	365	365	365	365	365
485	Discretionary Cash Flow per Share	527/478	na	0.08	-0.01	-0.03	0.01
486	Market Capitalisation (Millions)	478*480	0	0	0	0	0
487	Price / EBITDA per Share	480/514/478	na	0.0	0.0	0.0	0.0
488	Price / Discretionary Cash Flow per Share	480/527/478	na	0.0	0.0	0.0	0.0
489	Price / Free Cash Flow per Share	480/554/478	na	0.0	0.0	0.0	0.0
490	Price / Book	480/270/478					

OPEN UNIVERSITY FINANCIAL SPREADSHEET

Company Name:	Albert Fisher Group PLC	Date: 01-Jul-98
Business:	Food Processing and Distribution	Analyst: PAS
Currency:	Sterling Millions	
Domicile	UK	

	DERIVED CASH FLOW	Line Reference	30-Aug-93	30-Aug-94	30-Aug-95	30-Aug-96
510						
511						
512	NET OPERATING PROFIT (NOP)	336	47.9	40.9	38.2	47.6
513	+ Depreciation / Amortisation	320;321;322	15.5	16.6	18.2	19.4
514	EARNINGS BEFORE INTEREST, TAX, DEP'N & AMORT.(EBITDA)		63.4	57.5	56.4	67.0
515	+/- Δ Trade Receivables	117	(15.8)	(20.3)	(3.0)	4.6
516	+/- Δ Inventory	125	(5.7)	(22.4)	(5.3)	(13.4)
517	+/- Δ Trade Creditors	218	23.2	41.8	7.3	(15.7)
518	+/- Δ Accrued Expenses	219	6.9	0.7	4.8	1.6
519	+/- Δ Prepaid Expenses	136	(7.9)	(2.0)	2.9	1.9
520	Sub Total: Change Net Operating Assets		0.7	(2.2)	6.7	(21.0)
521	+/- Δ Other Current Assets	137, 135	2.0	(0.1)	(2.2)	2.5
522	+/- Δ Other Current Liabilities	220,226,227,234	17.6	(0.7)	7.8	11.8
523	OPERATING CASH FLOW (OCF)		83.7	54.5	68.7	60.3
524	- Taxes Paid	224,248,251,353..57,131,169	(13.4)	(12.0)	(3.9)	(6.7)
525	- Interest Paid	337,338	(20.2)	(11.3)	(13.7)	(18.4)
526	- Current Portion Long Term Debt & Leases	215,216	0.0	(36.5)	(74.1)	(28.6)
527	DISCRETIONARY CASH FLOW		50.1	(5.3)	(23.0)	6.6
528	- Dividends Paid	225,362...365	(24.8)	(23.1)	(26.6)	(26.8)
529	CASH FLOW BEFORE LONG TERM USES (CFBLTU)		25.3	(28.4)	(49.6)	(20.2)
530	- Expenditure on Property, Plant and Equipment	148,320,321,348,339,278,280,281	(35.6)	(56.3)	(33.5)	(46.5)
531	+ Proceeds from Sale of Property, Plant & Equip.	279	5.6	4.1	1.1	0.5
532	Subtotal Net Expenditure on PP&E		(30.0)	(52.2)	(32.4)	(46.0)
533	+/- Net Expenditure on Investments	333,343,349,153	4.4	0.6	(1.0)	4.9
534	+ Interest Received	340	0.0	0.0	0.0	0.0
535	+ Dividends Received	344	0.0	0.0	0.0	0.0
536	+/- Δ Intangibles	178,322	0.0	0.0	0.0	0.0
537	+/- Δ Other Long Term Assets	158,163,170,171,172	(0.3)	2.5	0.4	(0.3)
538	+/- Δ Other Long Term Liabilities	249	(4.7)	(2.1)	(1.6)	1.7
539	+/- Δ Provisions	233,257	0.0	0.0	0.0	0.0
540	+/- Δ Minority Interests	258,361,362	(2.2)	(0.0)	1.0	(0.0)
541	+/- Δ Reserves	264..268,280,281,367..372	(15.3)	(35.0)	11.2	124.5
542	+ Other Non-core Income	331,333,341,342,346,347	17.2	8.1	23.2	16.6
543	+/- Exceptional / Extraordinary Income or Expense	350,351,359,360	(15.4)	0.0	0.0	(151.0)
544	CASH FLOW AFTER INVESTING ACTIVITIES (CFAIA)		(21.0)	(106.5)	(48.8)	(69.8)
545	+/- Δ Share Capital	260..263,365	(84.5)	52.5	(30.1)	0.1
546	+/- Δ Long Term Debt	215,216,244	(55.5)	71.5	82.3	48.4
547	+/- Δ Short Term Debt	212..214	(1.5)	(6.2)	(1.1)	5.9
548	CASH FLOW AFTER FINANCING ACTIVITIES (CFAFA)		(162.5)	11.3	2.3	(15.4)
549	CHANGE IN CASH	111,112	162.5	(11.3)	(2.3)	15.4
550			0.0	0.0	0.0	0.0
551	**Adjusted Cash Flow Subtotals:**					
553	Operating Free Cash Flow (OFCF)	523-513+524	54.8	25.9	46.6	34.2
554	Free Cash Flow (FCF)	553+525	34.6	14.6	32.9	15.8
555	Residual Free Cash Flow (RFCF)	554+528	9.8	(8.5)	6.3	(11.0)
556	Adjusted Operating Cash Flow (AOCF)	514+520	64.1	55.3	63.1	46.0

OPEN UNIVERSITY FINANCIAL SPREADSHEET

Company Name:	Albert Fisher Group PLC	Date: 01-Jul-98
Business:	Food Processing and Distribution	Analyst: PAS
Currency:	Sterling Millions	
Domicile:	UK	

	BREAKDOWN BY DIVISION	30-Aug-92	30-Aug-93	30-Aug-94	30-Aug-95	30-Aug-96
610						
611	**SALES BY DIVISION**					
612	Division 1- European Food Processing		266.8	247.1	246.2	271.1
613	Division 2 - European Fresh Produce		408.5	478.0	373.0	390.5
614	Division 3 - European Seafood		126.3	165.9	304.6	396.3
615	Division 4 - North American Produce		360.5	481.9	183.9	181.5
616	Division 5					
617	Subtotal Continuing Operations	0.0	1,162.1	1,372.9	1,107.7	1,239.4
618	Discontinued Operations					
619	Other					
620	Other					
621	**TOTAL**	0.0	1,162.1	1,372.9	1,107.7	1,239.4
622	**% CHANGE IN SALES**					
623	Division 1- European Food Processing			(7.38%)	(0.36%)	10.11%
624	Division 2 - European Fresh Produce			17.01%	(21.97%)	4.69%
625	Division 3 - European Seafood			31.35%	83.60%	30.11%
626	Division 4 - North American Produce			33.68%	(61.84%)	(1.31%)
627	Division 5					
628	Subtotal Continuing Operations			18.14%	(19.32%)	11.89%
629	Discontinued Operations					
630	Other					
631	Other					
632	**TOTAL**			18.14%	(19.32%)	11.89%
633	**SALES BY DIVISION AS % OF TOTAL SALES**					
634	Division 1- European Food Processing		22.96%	18.00%	22.23%	21.87%
635	Division 2 - European Fresh Produce		35.15%	34.82%	33.67%	31.51%
636	Division 3 - European Seafood		10.87%	12.08%	27.50%	31.98%
637	Division 4 - North American Produce		31.02%	35.10%	16.60%	14.64%
638	Division 5					
639	Subtotal Continuing Operations		100.00%	100.00%	100.00%	100.00%
640	Discontinued Operations					
641	Other					
642	Other					
643	**TOTAL**		100.00%	100.00%	100.00%	100.00%
644	**NET OPERATING PROFIT BY DIVISION**					
645	Division 1- European Food Processing		13.7	13.5	12.1	19.4
646	Division 2 - European Fresh Produce		6.4	10.7	13.4	12.7
647	Division 3 - European Seafood		10.0	8.1	7.5	7.7
648	Division 4 - North American Produce		11.6	6.4	3.3	5.2
649	Division 5					
650	Subtotal Continuing Operations	0.0	41.7	38.7	36.3	45.0
651	Discontinued Operations					
652	Other					
653	Other					
654	**TOTAL**	0.0	41.7	38.7	36.3	45.0
655	**% CHANGE IN NET OPERATING PROFIT BY DIVISION**					
656	Division 1- European Food Processing			(1.46%)	(10.37%)	60.33%
657	Division 2 - European Fresh Produce			67.19%	25.23%	(5.22%)
658	Division 3 - European Seafood			(19.00%)	(7.41%)	2.67%
659	Division 4 - North American Produce			(44.83%)	(48.44%)	57.58%
660	Division 5					
661	Subtotal Continuing Operations			(7.19%)	(6.20%)	23.97%
662	Discontinued Operations					
663	Other					
664	Other					
665	**TOTAL**			(7.19%)	(6.20%)	23.97%
666	**NET OPERATING PROFIT % OF SALES BY DIVISION**					
667	Division 1- European Food Processing		5.13%	5.46%	4.91%	7.16%
668	Division 2 - European Fresh Produce		1.57%	2.24%	3.59%	3.25%
669	Division 3 - European Seafood		7.92%	4.88%	2.46%	1.94%
670	Division 4 - North American Produce		3.22%	1.33%	1.79%	2.87%
671	Division 5					
672	Subtotal Continuing Operations		3.59%	2.82%	3.28%	3.63%
673	Discontinued Operations					
674	Other					
675	Other					
676	**TOTAL**		3.59%	2.82%	3.28%	3.63%

APPENDIX 6   BLUE CIRCLE DERIVED CASH FLOW

OPEN UNIVERSITY FINANCIAL SPREADSHEET

Company Name:	Blue Circle Industries PLC	Date: 12-Jun-98	
Business:	Building Mat'ls & Property Dev't	Analyst: PAS	
Currency:	Sterling Millions		
Domicile	UK		

	DERIVED CASH FLOW	Line Reference	31-Dec-94	31-Dec-95	31-Dec-96	31-Dec-97
510						
511						
512	NET OPERATING PROFIT (NOP)	336	195.9	215.6	239.4	195.4
513	+ Depreciation / Amortisation	320;321;322	91.8	95.2	94.0	106.8
514	EARNINGS BEFORE INTEREST, TAX, DEP'N & AMORT.(EBITDA)		287.7	310.8	333.4	302.2
515	+/- Δ Trade Receivables	117	(8.2)	0.6	20.3	(39.6)
516	+/- Δ Inventory	125	7.5	(36.5)	23.6	(34.1)
517	+/- Δ Trade Creditors	218	6.7	7.6	(7.0)	(3.5)
518	+/- Δ Accrued Expenses	219	25.4	(7.4)	(7.0)	0.7
519	+/- Δ Prepaid Expenses	136	(3.4)	1.7	10.0	(5.8)
520	Sub Total: Change Net Operating Assets		28.0	(34.0)	39.9	(82.3)
521	+/- Δ Other Current Assets	137, 135	(2.8)	(21.0)	6.1	5.3
522	+/- Δ Other Current Liabilities	220,226,227,234	6.3	7.6	(2.1)	(8.3)
523	OPERATING CASH FLOW (OCF)		319.2	263.4	377.3	216.9
524	- Taxes Paid	224,248,251,353..57,131,169	(54.1)	(89.4)	(88.5)	(67.6)
525	- Interest Paid	337,338	(51.8)	(55.2)	(47.0)	(54.2)
526	- Current Portion Long Term Debt & Leases	215,216	(94.8)	(3.1)	(1.7)	(1.8)
527	DISCRETIONARY CASH FLOW		118.5	115.7	240.1	93.3
528	- Dividends Paid	225,362...365	(89.3)	(95.9)	(101.6)	(108.4)
529	CASH FLOW BEFORE LONG TERM USES (CFBLTU)		29.2	19.8	138.5	(15.1)
530	- Expenditure on Property, Plant and Equipment	148,320,321,348,339,278,280,281	(89.7)	(119.2)	(24.6)	(369.6)
531	+ Proceeds from Sale of Property, Plant & Equip.	279	41.3	20.8	22.4	27.1
532	Subtotal Net Expenditure on PP&E		(48.4)	(98.4)	(2.2)	(342.5)
533	+/- Net Expenditure on Investments	333,343,349,153	26.1	28.0	(13.0)	66.0
534	+ Interest Received	340	30.9	41.7	39.7	43.2
535	+ Dividends Received	344	20.9	28.7	25.4	31.3
536	+/- Δ Intangibles	178,322	0.0	0.0	0.0	0.0
537	+/- Δ Other Long Term Assets	158,163,170,171,172	(16.2)	0.3	(5.7)	(20.6)
538	+/- Δ Other Long Term Liabilities	249	26.9	9.9	5.6	16.3
539	+/- Δ Provisions	233,257	(10.8)	54.1	(40.4)	9.6
540	+/- Δ Minority Interests	258,361,362	(2.8)	(5.3)	(14.4)	(27.1)
541	+/- Δ Reserves	264..268,280,281,367..372	111.0	(5.0)	(118.9)	(111.4)
542	+ Other Non-core Income	331,333,341,342,346,347	(7.4)	5.2	9.3	5.1
543	+/- Exceptional / Extraordinary Inome or Expense	350,351,359,360	(43.2)	(0.7)	0.0	0.0
544	CASH FLOW AFTER INVESTING ACTIVITIES (CFAIA)		116.2	78.3	23.9	(345.2)
545	+/- Δ Share Capital	260..263,365	22.8	8.7	9.6	100.1
546	+/- Δ Long Term Debt	215,216,244	(125.6)	16.9	(40.5)	75.1
547	+/- Δ Short Term Debt	212..214	110.5	8.5	(87.3)	4.4
548	CASH FLOW AFTER FINANCING ACTIVITIES (CFAFA)		123.9	112.4	(94.3)	(165.6)
549	CHANGE IN CASH	111,112	(123.9)	(112.4)	94.3	165.6
550			0.0	0.0	0.0	0.0
551	**Adjusted Cash Flow Subtotals:**					
553	Operating Free Cash Flow (OFCF)	523-513+524	173.3	78.8	194.8	42.5
554	Free Cash Flow (FCF)	553+525	121.5	23.6	147.8	(11.7)
555	Residual Free Cash Flow (RFCF)	554+528	32.2	(72.3)	46.2	(120.1)
556	Adjusted Operating Cash Flow (AOCF)	514+520	315.7	276.8	373.3	219.9

REFERENCES

B800 *Foundations of Senior Management*, Book 14 The Marketing Environment.

Ball, R. (1995) 'Making accounting more international: why, how, and how far will it go?', *Journal of Applied Corporate Finance*, Fall.

Hawkins, D.R. (1993) 'Daimler-Benz: a US GAAP based stock', *Accounting Bulletin*, No. 19, 10 October.

Likierman, A. (1993) 'Performance indicators: 20 early lessons from managerial use', *Public Money and Management*, October/December.

Porter, M.E. (1979) 'How competitive forces shape strategy', *Harvard Business Review*, March/April.

Porter, M.E. (1985) *Competitive Advantage: Creating and sustaining superior performance*, The Free Press, New York.

Queens Moat Houses plc (1992) *Report and Accounts*.

Smith, P. (1993) 'Outcome-related performance indicators and organisational control in the public sector', *British Journal of Management*, Vol. 4, pp. 135–151.

Waller, D. (1979) 'International accounting standard wins recruits', *Corporate Finance*, August 1996.

Acknowledgements

Grateful acknowledgement is made to the following sources for permission to reproduce material in this unit:

Text

Extracts from auditors' reports, 1994, for Guinness Peat Aviation, reproduced by permission of GPA Group plc; Extracts from auditors' reports, 1996, for Eurotunnel plc Group, reproduced by permission of Eurotunnel plc Group; Extracts from the *Blue Circle Annual Report 1995*, reproduced by permission of Blue Circle Industries plc.

Figure

Figure 3.1: Reprinted by permission of *Harvard Business Review.* Exhibit from 'How competitive forces shape strategy', by Porter, M.E. March/April 1979. Copyright © 1979 by the President and Fellows of Harvard College; All rights reserved.

Cartoons

p. 9: Leo Cullum and *Harvard Business Review*, Vol. 74, No. 1, 1996; p. 11: The latest Alex collection, *Alex Feels the Pinch*, is published by Headline Book Publishing Ltd and is available in all major bookshops; p. 37: Nick Downes and *Harvard Business Review*, Vol. 69, No. 3, 1991; p. 50: Reproduced by kind permission of Punch 1977; p. 53: Leo Cullum and *Harvard Business Review*, Vol. 66, No. 5, 1988; p. 77: Leo Cullum and *Harvard Business Review*, Vol. 69, No. 1, 1991.

B821 FINANCIAL STRATEGY